REFLECTIONS

How twenty-six churches see their life and mission

Published for
The Inter-Church Process 'Not Strangers But Pilgrims'
by The British Council of Churches
2 Eaton Gate London SW1W 9BL
and The Catholic Truth Society,
38/40 Eccleston Square London SW1V 1PD

Notes on Statistics

Unless otherwise indicated, all figures have been taken from the 1985/86 **UK Christian Handbook** and are estimates for 1985.

Membership figures relate to the total number of adult (over 14) members/adherents in the UK. Definitions of membership vary according to the church denomination or religious group in question. Adult church membership is defined as appropriate to each particular group, so that, for example, the Electoral Roll (not to be confused with the Local Authority Electoral Roll) has been used for the Church of England, whilst estimates, comparable to the Protestant definitions of membership, have been made for the Roman Catholic Church. Where attendance figures are used, these are footnoted.

Ministers are full-time active clergy, or ordained officials, including those in administration.

Churches are those religious buildings in regular use, normally wholly owned by the organisations. Numbers of buildings do not necessarily correspond to the number of congregations or groups within the particular denomination.

ISBN 0–85169–112–9
Book design by Roger Dawson
Typeset by Chippendale Type, Otley, West Yorks.
Printed by Hutson Print Ltd., Warrington, Cheshire.
© 1986 Inter Church Process/British Council of Churches

Contents

Introduction

On the evening of 8 November 1985 in St Peter's Church, Eaton Square, a ceremony was held to celebrate the launch of the inter-church process **'Not Strangers But Pilgrims'**. During that ceremony representatives of the thirty-two participating Churches lit candles and placed them in a tray of earth. The candles burned side by side symbolising the undertaking given by those Churches to work side by side in prayer, study and discussion in this new initiative from that moment until the autumn of 1987.

'Not Strangers But Pilgrims' is then a process of prayer, study and dialogue between the vast majority of the Christian Churches in England, Scotland and Wales. It represents perhaps the most wide-ranging ecumenical initiative yet, not simply because of the number of participating Churches, but because the process has tried to include not only local level discussions and prayers but also the fruits of the formal international dialogues which have been taking place in recent years. The first results of these local discussions are to be published in a companion volume entitled **'Views from the Pews'**; the findings of the international dialogues and of other consultations in Britain and abroad will form the third volume with the title **'Observations'**.

This present volume, however, brings together the statements put forward by the participating Churches at national level in response to the question which is central to the whole process **'Not Strangers But Pilgrims'**:

> *"In your tradition and experience, how do you understand the nature and purpose of your Church (or Churches when the national body is a federation of local Churches)*
> *in relation to other Christian denominations*
> *and as we share in God's mission to the world?"*

It was in June 1985 that the participating Churches (listed on page 156) were asked to answer this question in a manner which 'includes the viewpoints of those concerned with mission, ministry and social responsibility as well as those concerned with faith and order'. The responses sought were to be 'provisional responses, drawn up by whatever means each Church chooses for the purpose of this process. It is not intended to seek statements formally approved by general Assemblies and Synods. Nevertheless they should be responses which members of that church would recognise as an expression of its self-understanding'. (Introductory Document, **'Not Strangers But Pilgrims'**, p9).

The responses received from the participating Churches are now presented in this volume. It is, I believe, a unique collection: churches confessing to one another, in charity and honesty, their self understanding and their reflections on their relationships with each other. As such it forms an important part of the first phase of **'Not Strangers But Pilgroms'** a phase of gathering together and listening to people's experience at many levels.

The second phase of the process which now lies ahead of us, is that of discernment and reflection. At every level, participants in this process are invited to open themselves to the faith of others and together to address those key issues which can be found in these pages. A series of Conferences have been planned for 1987 in which the experience of these discussions and prayer can be brought together, first of all at the level of each country and then at the level of this island as a whole.

That lies ahead. **'Not Strangers But Pilgrims'** is a process and not a pre-determined programme. We pray that we are being led by the Holy Spirit and that we are open to his guidance.

It has been my duty to bring these documents together. It has been a rich and rewarding experience for me. I hope that all who take up this book may find in it both support and challenge as together we seek to be obedient to the will of our one Lord: 'that they all may be one'.

V. Nichols

African Methodist Episcopal Church

Members: 200 *Ministers: 2* *Churches: 2**

* Not owned by the Church but shared churches
Figures supplied by the African Methodist Episcopal Church

Statement of Belief

Tradition and experience: we believe in the Oneness of Christ being the sure Foundation, therefore all Christian Churches should be one foundation in Jesus Christ Our Lord. Real togetherness is vital in ecumenical terms for the christian faith. Traditionally the church, my church, is a family of World Methodism; our heritage involves the struggle for freedom of worship in simplicity and truth, Christ being the Way, the Light and Truth. This is our Christian experience.

As we share in God's mission to the world the Person of Christ as Missioner proclaims His work amongst men and calls his disciples to continue His mission of the gospel with love, peace and human awareness at all times. "Let brotherly love continue": a true Theology of Christ.

Ecumenically yours,
The African Methodist Episcopal Church.

The Mission and Purpose of the Church

Each local Church of the African Methodist Episcopal Church shall be engaged in carrying out the spirit of the original Free African Society out of which the A.M.E. Church evolved, that is, to seek out and save the lost and serve the needs through a continuing program of: (1) preaching the gospel, (2) feeding the hungry, (3) clothing the naked, (4) housing the homeless, (5) cheering the fallen, (6) providing jobs for the jobless, (7) administering to the needs of those in prisons, hospitals, nursing homes, asylums and mental institutions, senior citizens' homes, caring for the sick, the shut-in, the mentally and socially disturbed, and (8) encouraging thrift and economic advancement.

DOCTRINAL AFFIRMATIONS

Section 1. Articles of Religion

1. Of faith in The Holy Trinity

There is but one living and true God, everlasting, without body on parts, of infinite power, wisdom, and goodness, the Maker and Preserver of all things visible and invisible, and in unity of this Godhead, there are three persons of one substance, power and eternity: The Father, the Son, and the Holy Ghost.

2. Of the Word or Son of God Who Was Made Very Man

The Son, who is the Word of the Father, the very and eternal God, of one substance with the Father, took man's nature in the womb of the blessed Virgin, so that two whole and perfect natures, that is to say the Godhead and manhood were joined together in one person, never to be divided; whereof is one Christ, very God, and very man, who truly suffered, was crucified, dead and buried, to reconcile his Father to us and to be sacrificed, not only for original guilt, but also for the actual sins of men.

3. Of the Resurrection of Christ

Christ did truly rise again from the dead, and took again his body with all things appertaining to the perfection of man's nature, wherewith he ascended into heaven, and there sitteth until he returns to judge all men at the last day.

4. Of the Holy Ghost

The Holy Ghost, proceeding from the Father and the Son, is of one substance, majesty and glory with the Father and the Son, very and eternal God.

5. The Sufficiency in the Holy Scriptures For Salvation

The Holy Scriptures contain all things necessary to salvation, so that whatsoever is not read therein, nor may be proved thereby, is not to be required of any man that it should be believed an article of faith, or be thought requisite or necessary to salvation. By the name of the Holy Scriptures, we do understand those canonical books of the Old and New Testaments of whose authority was never any doubt in the church.

The names of the canonical books: Genesis, Exodus, Leviticus, Numbers, Deuteronomy, Joshua, Judges, Ruth, The First Book of Samuel, The second Book of Samuel, The First Book of Kings, The Second Book of Kings, The First Book of Chronicles, The Second Book of Chronicles, The Book of Ezra, The Book of Nehemiah, The Book of Esther, The Book of Job, The Psalms, The Proverbs, Ecclesiastes (or the Preacher), Cantia (or Songs of Solomon), Four Prophets, the Greater, Twelve Prophets, the Less.
All of the books of the New Testament, as they are commonly received, we do receive and account Canonical.

6. Of The Old Testament

The Old Testament is not contrary to the New, for both in the Old and New Testaments everlasting life is offered to mankind by Christ, who is the only mediator between God and man, being both God and Man. Wherefore they are not to be heard who feign that the old fathers did look only for transitory promises. Although the law given from God by Moses, as touching ceremonies and rites, doth not bind Christians, nor ought the civil precepts thereof of necessity by received in any commonwealth, yet notwithstanding, no Christian whatsoever is free from the obedience of the commandments which are called moral.

7. Of the Original or Birth Sin

Original sin standeth not in the following of Adam (as the Pelagians do vainly talk), but it is the corruption of the nature of every man that naturally is engendered of the offspring of

Adam, whereby man is very far gone from orginal righteousness and of his own nature inclined to evil, and that continually.

8. Of Free Will
The condition of man after the fall of Adam is such that he cannot turn and prepare himself by his own natural strength and works to faith and calling upon God: wherefore we have no power to do good works, pleasant and acceptable to God without the grace of God, by Christ preventing us, that we may have a good will and working with us when we have that good will.

9. Of the Justification of man
We are accounted righteous before God only for the merit of our Lord and Savior Jesus Christ by faith, and not for our own works and deserving; wherefore, that we are justified by faith only is a most wholesome doctrine and very full of comfort.

10. Of Good Works
Although good works, which are the fruits of faith and follow after justification, cannot put away our sins and endure the severity of God's judgment, yet are they pleasing and acceptable to God in Christ, and spring out of a true and lively faith, insomuch that by them a lively faith may be as evidently known, as a tree is discerned by its fruits.

11. Of Works of Supererogation
Voluntary works, besides, over and above God's command-ments, which are called works of supererogation, cannot be taught without arrogance and impiety. For by them men do declare that they do not only render unto God as much as they are bound to do, but they do more for His sake than of bounden duty is required.

Whereas, Christ saith plainly: "When ye have done all that is commanded you, say we are unprofitable servants."

12. Of Sin After Justification
Not every sin willingly commited after justification is the sin against the Holy Ghost, and unpardonable. Wherefore, the grant of repentance is not to be denied to such as fall into sin

after justification. After we have received the Holy Ghost, we may depart from grace given and fall into sin, and by the grace of God rise again and amend our lives. And therefore they are to be condemned who say they can do no more sin as long as they live here, or deny the place of forgiveness to such as truly repent.

13. Of the Church
The Visible Church of Christ is a congregation of faithful men and women in which the pure Word of God is preached, and the sacraments duly administered according to Christ's ordinance, in all those things that of necessity are requisite to the same.

14. Of Purgatory
The Romish doctrine concerning purgatory, pardon, worshipping and adoration, as well of images as of relics, and also invocation of saints is a fond thing vainly invented and grounded on no warrant of Scripture but repugnant to the Word of God.

15. Of Speaking in the Congregation in Such a Tongue as the people Understand
It is a thing plainly repugnant to the Word of God, and the custom, of the primitive Church, to have public prayer in the Church or to minister the sacraments in a tongue not understood by the people. (In all places, ministers should strive to conduct services in the language of the people).

16. Of the Sacraments
Sacraments ordained of Christ are not only badges or tokens of Christian men's profession, but rather they are certain signs of grace and God's will toward us, by which he doth work invisibly in us, and doth not only quicken but also strengthen and conform our faith in Him.

There are two Sacraments ordained of Christ our Lord in the Gospel; that is to say, Baptism and the Supper of the Lord or Holy Communion.

Those five commonly called Sacraments, that is to say Conformation, Penance, Orders, Matrimony and Extreme Unction are not to be counted for Sacraments of the Gospel, being such as have partly grown out of the CORRUPT following of the Apostles and partly are states of life allowed in the Scriptures – but yet have not the like nature of Baptism and the Lord's Supper, because they have not any visible sign or ceremony ordained of God.

The Sacraments were not ordained of Christ to be gazed upon, or to be carried about; but that we should duly use them. And in such only as worthily received the same, they have a wholesome effect or operation; but they that receive them unworthily purchase to themselves condemnation as St. Paul saith, 1 Cor. 11:29.

17. Of Baptism
Baptism is not only a sign of profession and mark of difference, whereby Christians are distinguished from others that are not baptized, but it is also a sign of regeneration or the new birth. The baptism of infants and young children is to be retained in the church.

18. Of The Lord's Supper
The Supper of the Lord is not only a sign of love that Christians ought to have among themselves one to another, but rather is a Sacrament of our redemption by Christ's death; insomuch that, to such as rightly, worthily, and with faith receive the same, the bread which we break is a partaking of the body of Christ, and likewise the cup of blessing is a partaking of the blood of Christ.

Transubstantiation, or the change of the substance of bread and wine in the Supper of our Lord, cannot be proved by Holy Writ, but is repugnant to the plain words of Scripture, overthroweth the nature of a Sacrament, and hath given occasion to many superstitions.

The body of Christ is given, received and eaten in the Supper, only after a heavenly and spiritual manner. And the means whereby the body of Christ is received and eaten in the Supper, is faith. The Sacrament of the Lord's Supper, is not by Christ's ordinance reserved, carried about, lifted up, or worshipped.

19. Of Both Kinds
The cup of the Lord is not to be denied to the lay people, for both the parts of the Lord's Supper, by Christ's ordinance and

commandment, ought to be administered to all Christians alike.

20. Of the One Oblation of Christ Finished Upon the Cross

The offering of Christ once made is that perfect redemption, propitiation, and satisfaction for all the sins of the whole world, both original and actual; and there is none other satisfaction for sin but that alone. Wherefore, the sacrifice of masses, in which it is commonly said that the priest doth offer Christ, for the quick and the dead, to have remission of pain or guilt, it is a blasphemous fable and dangerous deceit.

21. Of the Marriage of Ministers

The ministers of Christ are not commanded by God's law, either to vow the estate of single life or to abstain from marriage; therefore it is lawful for them, as for all Christians, to marry at their own discretion, as they shall judge the same to serve best to godliness.

22. Of the Rites and Ceremonies of Church

It is not necessary that rites and ceremonies should in all places be the same or exactly alike, for they have been always different, and may be changed according to the diversity of countries, times, and men's manners, so long as nothing be ordained against God's word. Whosoever, through his private judgment, willingly and purposely doth openly break the rites and ceremonies of the Church to which he belongs, which are not repugnant to the word of God and are ordained and approved by common authority, ought to be rebuked openly, that others may fear to do the like, as one that offendeth against the common order of the Church and woundeth the conscience of weak brethren.

Every particular Church may ordain, change, or abolish rites and ceremonies so that all things may be done to edification.

23. Of the Rule of the United States of America

The President, the Congress, the general Assemblies, the Government of the United States of America, according to the division of power, made to them by the Constitution and the Councils of State as the delegates of the people, are the rulers of the United States of America, and by the Constitution of their respective States. And said States are a sovereign and independent nation and ought not to be subject to any foreign jurisdiction.*

24. Of Christian men's Goods
The riches and goods of Christians are not common as touching the right, the title, and possession of the same as some do falsely boast. Notwithstanding, every man ought to use all goods as a trust from God, of such things as he possesseth, liberally to give alms to the poor, according to his ability.

25. Of a Christian man's Oath
We confess that vain and rash swearing is forbidden Christian men, by our Lord Jesus Christ and James His apostle, but we judge that the Christian religion doth not prohibit, that a man may swear when the magistrate requireth in a cause of faith and charity, or it be done according to the prophet's teaching in justice, judgment, and truth.

Obedience to Civil Government, however, is one of the principal duties of all men, and was honored by our Lord and His Apostles. Though differing in form and policy, all righteous governments rightfully command the obedience, loyalty, support, and defense of all Christian men and women as that they control and protect.

Section 2. Special Declaration on Apostolic Succession

Whereas, We have heard with deep regret the dogma of Apostolic Succession and the distinct and separate priesthood of the ministry preached in our pulpit and:
Whereas, There are those among us members of this body who are said to be seeking reordination at the hands of the Episcopal Bishops, and Bishops of the Protestant Episcopal Church.
Whereas, We have strong reasons for believing that what is thus reported has some foundation in fact, therefore be it
Resolved, By this, the Eighteenth General Conference now assembled, that we set forth the following declarations and that any person or persons who are not in harmony with the same or cannot subscribe thereto are hereby declared out of harmony

with the standards of Methodism and are liable to impeachment for propagating error and sowing dissention to wit:

First – we hold and believe that there is no separate priesthood under the Christian symbol set over the Church. That the sacerdotal theory of Christian ministry is a dishonor to our Lord Jesus and is especially condemned by the tenor of the Epistle to the Hebrews.

Second – That while there is a separate ministry in the New Testament representing the universal priesthood or membership of the Church, yet as has been affirmed above, each and every member is a king and priest under God.

Third – That we recognize the two orders and the one office in our church to be the regularly ordained ministry, and that we are satisfied with the ordinations of the same, holding it to be valid and true in every respect.

Fourth – That the doctrine of Apostolic Succession, according to our belief as Methodists, is erroneous. That there is an uninterrupted succession of ministers which the divine eye can trace up to the Apostolic times, there can be no doubt. But it is utterly impossible to prove that in any part of the world there is a ministry that can trace its orders up through episcopal hands to the Apostles.

Fifth – "That the Apostles had and could have no successors from the fact that their authority, indicated in two ways, was first to teach Christianity by words and writing, for which they had the gift of inspiration in a special sense; and secondly, to found the church, for which they had the power of the keys of binding and loosing, that is, of uttering unchangeable decrees of ecclesiastical government; that a succession of such men would not have been in harmony with the known will of Christ."

Baptist Union of Great Britain and Ireland

Members: 148,000   *Ministers: 1,360*   *Churches: 1,820*

Living with Tensions

Introduction

Like all Christian denominations Baptists bear the scars and glories of their history. They have become what they are as a result of various influences and events, brought about by human sin and divine grace and responded to with a mixture of faithfulness and disobedience. They would claim to have been subject to the commanding voice and gracious pressure of God in Christ. They are obliged to admit that other siren voices have not always gone unheeded.

In seeking to express their understanding of the nature and role of the church in relation to other Christian denominations and in the light of God's mission to the world they recognise that they live with tensions. These are expounded in the following sections:-

1. Church and World: The Tension of Mission.
2. Church and Churches: The Tension of Unity.
3. Church and Churchmanship: The Tension within.

Their prayer is that tensions may be creative rather than divisive, leading to a deeper self-understanding and a truer mutual understanding in dialogue with others.

1. Church and World: The Tension of Mission

Baptist churches, when they are true to their theological heritage, understand themselves to be believers with a mission. The call to be a fellowship of believers, a company of the committed, a society of saints, is held to be according to the genuine pattern of apostolic living and New Testament order. This is written deep in their history, though with such an understanding they must confess to being imperfect representatives of the Kingdom.

Conversion, personal faith, commitment and discipleship stand as a firm if eroded boundary line between world and church. Believers' baptism marks the decisive step from one to the other, with immersion symbolising the spiritual death and resurrection through which Christ brings the believer into the new life of the Kingdom.

This fact inevitably colours their understanding of the purpose and mission of the church. Churches are called to be visible communities of the forgiven and redeemed. Evangelism thus becomes a primary concern. The Declaration of Principle for churches in membership of the Baptist Union of Great Britain and Ireland brings these two emphases together in the following words:-

> "Christian Baptism is the immersion in water into the Name of the Father, the Son, and the Holy Ghost, of those who have professed repentance towards God and faith in our Lord Jesus Christ who 'died for our sins according to the Scriptures; was buried, and rose again the third day'.

> "It is the duty of every disciple to bear personal witness to the Gospel of Jesus Christ, and to take part in the evangelization of the world."

Most Baptists therefore would readily affirm that the church exists for mission, but behind their unity would be hidden significant divergence in expectation. For some mission would be equated with evangelism or certainly dominated by it. For others evangelism would be seen as by no means the sum of mission. Ministering to human need, washing the feet of the world, actively seeking the welfare of the city, standing in solidarity with the poor and oppressed, interceding or speaking and acting prophetically about crucial national and political issues – all these would be broadly believed to be an important part of the church's mission. It belongs to Christian discipleship to seek above all else the reign of God, as an inescapable implication of the Gospel.

Here is the point of tension. For where the Gospel is understood as essentially a message of personal redemption there is a strong tendency to give primacy to salvation over service. From this perspective some Baptists have tended to view with some ambivalence an emphasis on mission that highlights the transformation of society and its institutions and structures. Modern theology of the cosmic Christ whose purpose is to bring all things into perfect harmony in Himself has challenged such restricted individualism. Likewise contemporary ecumenism has reminded Baptists of wider understandings of mission within society.

This fundamental unity of the personal and corporate, salvation and service, spiritual and political, has never been totally absent. A view of mission which includes both the transform-ation of the individual and the transformation of society and its institutions arises from a belief in the Lordship of Christ which is expressed in baptism and which includes both the personal and the corporate. It takes seriously the nature of sin as affecting both individuals and principalities and powers, and it sees redemption not only as giving freedom from guilt and sin but also from any injustice which threatens the dignity of any human being. The terms Dissenter, Noncomformist, Free Churches all represent this radical criticism of society in the name of the Gospel, which extends to both church and state, and is an attempt to safeguard the Crown Rights of the Redeemer. Maybe it has been less evident because the historical roots of Baptists were in the repressed fringes of society without access to the levers of power. Their people consequently formed covenanted communities of separatist believers. Under the shadow of a national church with both privilege and responsibility for society through the parish system, Baptists naturally developed the concepts of the church gathered in faith and worship and scattered for evangelism. They would believe this to be a distinctive emphahsis to be shared with others. At the same time they must confess that they are learning with others their corporate and community responsibility, never to be separated from the crucial conflict between sin and grace in the human heart and will.

2. Church and Churches: The Tension of Unity

Baptist churches understand themselves to be local covenanted communities under the Lordship of Christ, fellowships gathered locally under the Gospel heard and obeyed. The rule of Christ as Head of the church is exercised and experienced when believers meet together face to face for mutual discernment under the guidance of the Spirit. So Christ is understood to rule through the church meeting. The Declaration of Principle states that:-

> "Our Lord and Saviour Jesus Christ, God manifest in the flesh, is the sole and absolute authority in all matters pertaining to faith and practice, as revealed in the Holy Scriptures, and that each Church has liberty, under the guidance of the Holy Spirit, to interpret and administer His Laws."

Theologically the church meeting is to be understood as a natural outcome of corporate worship where the Word is proclaimed and a response demanded. In practice it must be admitted that it has all too often been allowed to degenerate into a routine business meeting little different from a human democracy. A contemporary challenge is to rediscover the scriptural and theological understanding of the company of believers met with Christ in the midst as their Head.

A statement approved by the Council of the Baptist Union of Great Britain and Ireland in March 1948 declared:

> "Although Baptists have for so long held a position separate from that of other communions, they have always claimed to be part of the one holy catholic church of our Lord Jesus Christ. They believe in the catholic church as the holy society of believers in our Lord Jesus Christ, which He founded, of which He is the only Head, and in which He dwells by His Spirit – so that though manifested in many communions, it is yet one in Him."

This embodied the conviction expressed in the reply of the Annual Assembly of 1926 to the Lambeth Appeal.

Thus Baptists are not able to accept that their understanding of the church is a denial of catholicity or a failure to perceive the wholeness and universality of the church of God. They would point to the pervasive missionary concern which has characterised their life since the time of William Carey. This has focussed them on world horizons and led to their partnership with the Christian church in many lands. Similarly local churches have for centuries practised interdependence which has found expression in Associations regionally and Unions nationally (e.g. the Baptist Union of Wales, the Baptist Union of Scotland, and the Baptist Union of Great Britain and Ireland). Because the one church of Christ finds visible embodiment in the local church, Baptist churches see this mutual interconnectedness as arising from and always returning to the local church. Associations and Unions have no final authority over the local fellowship.

They do not deny that the Lord of the Church may and can and does speak or act through wider experiences of churchmanship. They retain, however, a strong conviction that recognition of that speech and action, and the obedience prompted thereby, must remain where locally the one church finds its visible expression, the covenanted community living under the Word and around the Table.

This perspective owes something to the complexities of history. It reflects the pattern of persecuted minorities reading the New Testament through the lens of experience. Yet it is also believed to constitute a coherent directing vision which Baptists have implemented in changing ways through changing times. Agencies for united action have been created to meet new needs. New patterns of ministry have been initiated to respond to new challenges or to provide wider bounds of oversight. But multiple orders of ministry have never been allowed to overshadow the one apostolic ministry of Word and Sacrament, deemed to belong to the health and wholeness of the gathered fellowship of believers within which a diversity of gifts for mutual ministering is bestowed.

This perspective also pinpoints the possibilities and problems for Baptists of relationships with other Christian denominations. They have felt free to recognise and welcome ministers and members of other churches on the simple basis of Christian profession and discipleship. They have readily acknowledged other Christian communions as churches where Christ reigns through the Gospel. Issues of church order and ministry have seldom presented substantial barriers to intercommunion or to common action in witness and service, although it must be acknowledged that some Baptists have refused to share in these ways with those whom they consider to be 'non-evangelical'.

It is at the point where unity, understood as the bringing together of denominations into one visible and institutional body, controls the agenda that two basic problems arise.

(a) That the unity of the church should be a visible unity is not widely disputed. The impasse arises when the model of unity invariably assumed is quite other than the model of churchmanship by which Baptists live. Where the controlling unit is the nation, or the model is hierarchical or pyramidal, or the national or regional level is the dominant centre, Baptists find themselves facing an understanding of the church not relatively but totally different from their own.

(b) It is a longstanding assumption that Baptist churchmanship (traditionally described as congregationalism) is really in essence no more than one distinctive and valuable component to be preserved and brought into what must ultimately be for all Christians an understanding of the church more comprehensive than that which any communion now possesses. Such an assumption wholly fails to grasp that the debate is about radically different total concepts of the church which have inescapable implications for the whole shape of the whole church.

Even behind these two problems there may lurk divergent ideas of how someone becomes a Christian and what a Christian is.

It is therefore no accident that Baptist ecumenical involvement has long been substantial in relation to such bodies as the Free Church Federal Council and the British and World Councils of Churches, whilst at the same time national unity proposals have

in general generated less enthusiasm than do ecumenical
ventures at local level.

3. Church and Churchmanship: The Tension Within

Self-understanding is easiest when boundaries are plain and
distinction from others is clear. Such a situation has existed for
Baptists in the past when separatism was at its peak. But for a
variety of reasons the contemporary situation is somewhat
confused and it would be difficult to describe Baptist identity in
a way that would command total assent within the
denomination.

For example, the social changes and historical pressures
through which they have passed in their journeying have led to
an inheritance of tangled traditions which have lived on within
them. Thus they are heirs to the hostilities which marked their
seventeenth century origins, to the renewal which was the fall-
out from the eighteenth century Evangelical Revival, to the
revulsion prompted by the nineteenth century Oxford
Movement in the Church of England and to the confidence
created in them when civil and religious disabilities were
eventually removed.

Various streams of life contributed to the formation of the
Baptist Union – Calvinism and Arminianism, General Baptists,
Particular Baptists and General Baptists of the New Connexion.
Their theological differences have never been wholly reconciled
and occasionally emerge in both ecclesiastical and theological
debate.

New developments in these ever-changing times are yet
another factor affecting contemporary Baptist self-understanding. Modern trends in biblical and theological scholarship
have brought tensions not easily overcome. At present these
differences seem to have become sharpened. Ecumenical
developments have inevitably removed familiar frontiers and
old denominational landmarks, a fact welcomed by some but
felt to be threatening by others. So local church responses to
ecumenism are sometimes out of sympathy with the Union's
continuing commitment to membership of the WCC and

BCC. More recently still has come the new pentecostalism of the charismatic movement, and in particular the move towards authoritarian presbyteral government of those committed to the Restoration Principles of the House Church movement.

All these factors have led to a situation in which searching questions are being asked about the essence of the particular identity of Baptist churches. Only when that is more clearly understood will there be a strong self-consciousness to enable Baptists unitedly to relate with conviction to others.

The present danger is that separate streams may be formed of those who seek a restoration of one biblical or theological stream instead of embracing the wide diversity of understanding which comes from our history. It is essential that evangelical substance, congregational ordering, committed discipleship and missionary concern remain the central principles. There will probably remain the long-standing tension between independence and inter-dependence, but it is to be hoped that this will be creative rather than disruptive. If it is, Baptists will be able with gladness and genuine commitment to seek with all God's people His purpose for them in Christ. They will need to go on exploring their own position but that will be best done in fellowship with others, and with the prayer that they may hear what the Spirit is saying to the churches.

It is their conviction that united action to deal with the needs and problems of the modern world and a common voice against all that is seen to be contrary to God's will must not be delayed until theological and ecclesiastical exploration is complete. In fact, that very exploration may become more fruitful as all the churches discover closer bonds through sharing God's mission to the world.

In that faith and hope they offer this self-portrait to themselves and to others.

April 1986

Christian Brethren

Members: 64,000   *Ministers: 200*   *Churches: 1,560*

The Nature and Purpose of the Church

The Christian fellowships known as Brethren owe their origins to a spontaneous movement of the Spirit in the early years of the nineteenth century, in a not dissimilar fashion to the Methodist societies of the eighteenth century. They began as liberating communities of believers who wished to meet with one another on the sole basis of their common faith in Christ and without denominational constraints on their unity.

These churches are now worldwide in extent and conduct their testimonies as unfederated, autonomous local congregations which are independent of any other governance than that exercised in the leadership of local elders recognised as such by the members themselves.

The Nature of the Church

The Scripture teaches that the Church is the instrument in God's plan to bring all creation together with Christ as Head of all things. As the Body of Christ, the Christian community is joined to Christ and works together with Him to fulfil the economy of God.

This community is essentially a charismatic body and not an institutional organisation, established by the grace of God and built up by the gifts of grace bestowed sovereignly by the Holy Spirit. It is the fellowship of all true believers through time and, as the People of God, they form the 'ecclesia' – the called-out and called-together Church of God.

The people of God are called to worship together in fellowship (*koinonia*) with the preaching of the Word and in the keeping of the Ordinances, to serve (*diakonia*) God and one another in Christ and in servanthood towards the world, to bear witness (*marturia*) in proclamation (*evangelism*) and by deeds (*caritas*). It is this model of a holy, catholic and apostolic church that Brethren fellowships seek to follow humbly in the steps of the Master. Christians are to be 'salt' to preserve and 'light' to illumine the dark world in which they serve but do not become identified with its evil forces.

This N.T. model of the Church as a charismatic community has been rediscovered by K. Rahner in his **Church From the Roots**, a basal ecclesia defining as an authenitic church any place "where two or three are gathered together in my Name" with the promise of the Lord's presence.

The Ministry of the Church

In a grass roots, people centred fellowship, the model of the Body of Christ in which "the whole body... joined together... grows and builds itself up in love, as each part does its work..." is one which declares the shared ministry of all members, serving one another. The diversity of gifts exhibited in any one local congregation demonstrates the nature of unity in fellowship. "Where the life of the local church is characterised by love, reconciliation, forgiveness, mutual acceptance and accountability, and when each member freely uses his Spirit-given ministry for the good of the others, the basis is laid for the spontaneous expansion of the Gospel..."
(C. Rene Padilla).

The gifts of the Spirit to the local church whether in persons (*domata*) or in functions (*charismata*) are to be identified, encouraged and developed for the church's mission to others. These are widely distributed in the *laos* of God and Brethren churches can see no scriptural basis for making a distinction between clergy and laity in God's service. Ordination to His work is the operation of the Holy Spirit which the churches receive and confirm in their midst.

It is also clear from the N.T. Scriptures that the local church leadership was always in the plural. We never find a presbyter in the singular; he is always a member of a team. Commenting on Ephesians 4:12, Michael Harper in his book **Let My People Grow** states that the five aspects of ministry cited are parts of all true Christian leadership. They are not all likely to be found in one man but they should be found in every healthy congregation. The balance includes: the apostolic role, following Christ-centred kerygmatic teachings in an out-reaching, pioneering mission; the prophetic role, quietly listening to God to be able to speak with insight into a situation; the pastoral role, knowing the sheep by name and caring for them as the 'under shepherds' of the Church; the teaching role for the church's growth into the maturity of Christ; the evangelistic role that the world might know the saving work of Christ.

Authority to undertake these ministries is given by God alone and not by human systems, and is received corporately by the local church to be shared by the members acting in Christ's Name. These are the underlying principles of church ministry which are follwed by Brethren assemblies.

The Unity of the Church
This is subordinate to the prior unity of the believer in Christ. As an individual confessing faith in his Saviour and Lord, he becomes *ipso facto* a member of the Body of Christ, the universal Church without regard to historical or denominational varieties. The choice which a new believer makes in joining with a particular manifestation of the local church will turn on a number of different factors at work. Hopefully, he will study the Scriptures on the matter and allow the Holy Spirit to lead him where He wills.

The existence of major institutional structures which have added denominational conditions to church membership complicates the issue of unity. It may well be that some modification or even in someways, dismantling of such structures will be necessary before the whole People of God can rejoice together in their one Lord and meet with one another at His Table. Philip Hughes, writing two decades ago, says: "...the basis then of all genuine Christian unity already exists, since all who are incorporated into Christ by grace... are unescapably one with each other. One of the greater threats to the Church's spirituality today is the pursuit of over-organisation as a means to the achievement of unity…".

True and effective ecumenism is most evident in our churches at the local levels of action – in joint mission and evangelism, in shared social services to the community around us, in political concern for righteous living and in many other ways. These 'bindings together' are best left at this level where the shared belief and objectives are likely to be higher than those of national scale activities.

The Hope of the Church
The Church is essentially a pilgrim community. Whilst established in the 'here and now' and with a mission to the world at large, it is also a Church in prospect awaiting the return of its Lord to be united with it as His Bride. Then will come the manifestation of the Kingdom of God and of his Christ to whom the nations will bend the knee and acknowledge his eternal Lordship. The Kingdom of God which is presently within the hearts of the faithful will be set up in justice and equity for all to see.

It is this eschatological picture which informs the expectations of Brethren churches across the world, in company with many biblical communities of all kinds. Their activities in prophetic ministry, in servanthood to others, in pastoral caring for a world in need are motivated by this drive to evangelise and to nurture in the faith. Their missionary enterprise is considerable in other lands and at home. As individual believers, they take part in many works of faith and charity, nationally and internationally, knowing that they will give an account of their stewardship in the Day of the Lord.

A pilgrim church is of necessity a changing and a growing church; it is never satisified with its achievements or becomes embedded in the world's affairs. It is truly an *ecclesia reformata et semper reformanda*. There is no ground for standing still as the Holy Spirit is allowed to lead us into new truth in Christ.

J. Boyes
April 1986

Church of England

Members: 1,725,000   *Ministers: 12,100*   *Churches: 16,700*

Response of Church of England to Not Strangers, But Pilgrims

1. "The Church of England is part of the One, Holy, Catholic and Apostolic Church, worshipping the one true God, Father, Son and Holy Spirit. She professes the faith uniquely revealed in the Holy Scriptures and set forth in the catholic creeds, which faith the Church is called upon to proclaim afresh in each generation. Led by the Holy Spirit, she has borne witness to Christian truth in her historic formularies, the Thirty-nine Articles of Religion, the Book of Common Prayer, and the Ordering of Bishops, Priests and Deacons." Every bishop, priest and deacon of the Church of England has to affirm his loyalty to this inheritance of faith as his "inspiration and guidance under God in bringing the grace and truth of Christ to this generation and making Him known to those in (his) care".

Preface to the Declaration of Assent

The Nature of the Church

The Church is One
2. The Church of England believes that it is part of the one, holy, catholic and apostolic Church. It has never claimed to be the whole of the Church. The classical Anglican theologian, Richard Hooker, described the Church universal as a great ocean, which was divided into various local seas. Every sea was linked to every other sea in the ocean, but each one had its local characteristics. There was, for example, a Church of the German people, a Church of the French people, and a Church of the English people. Ideally all should be in communion with one another.

Universal unity

3. The universal outworking of this concept of unity ran into difficulties when it became clear that there were grave and continuing differences dividing the Church of England from the Church of Geneva, for example, on the one hand or from the Church of Spain on the other. However, the Church of England did not seriously begin to come to terms in practice with the issue of universal unity until other Anglican Churches arose overseas and became indigenous and autonomous. There are now 28 such self-governing Churches or Provinces, owing a common allegiance to Jesus Christ as Head of the Church, and united in a common order based on the Lambeth Quadrilateral (the Holy Scripture, the catholic creeds, the Sacraments of Baptism and Holy Communion, and the historic episcopate).

4. The unity of the Anglican Communion has been maintained for the past 100 years by regular meetings of bishops at the Lambeth Conferences every 10 years. More recently the Anglican Consultative Council, comprising bishops, priests and laypeople from the various provinces of the Communion, has attempted to draw it more closely together at a time when its unity is threatened by divisions, for example, over the rightness of ordaining or not ordaining women to the priesthood and episcopate. In this situation the Archbishop of Canterbury serves as a focus of unity throughout the Anglican Communion, but he has no legal authority in other provinces.

Unity in England

5. Within England there was an attempt to make the Church of England the one and only Church. Successive governments passed *Acts of Uniformity* to force people to belong. Together with this, particularly under the Supreme Governorship of Queen Elizabeth I, every effort was made to adopt a church order and outline a doctrine which could comprehend all English people within one Church. (The reason for this was not simply religious and Christian, but also political and diplomatic. Unity in religious persuasion was seen as strengthening political cohesion and loyalty.)

6. This attempt at conformity and comprehensiveness in the

English post-Reformation Church soon failed. There were Roman Catholics who never conformed, and very soon there were Presbyterian and Independent dissenters too. It took some time for the English State to take cognisance of these other Churches in England and to accord their members and ministers full freedom and rights. It has also taken the Church of England a long time to recognise these Churches as partners in mission. The Church of England has never questioned the validity of the ministry of the Roman Catholic and Orthodox Churches. In this century the Church of England, while itself continuing to insist on the historic episcopate as a sign and means of unity, has been at pains also to affirm the spiritual reality and efficacy of the Free Churches and their ministries.

7. To this day, however, the Church of England believes that it has a special pastoral responsibility for all people in this country, whether they call themselves Anglicans or not. Virtually every corner of England is in a diocese and in a parish, and the people who live there are committed by the bishop to the spiritual care of a particular priest. Each diocese has considerable autonomy to pursue its own policies. It used to be said that the Church of England was not one Church, but 43 separate churches. This has become less true since the adoption of Synodical Government in 1970.

The Church is Holy
8. The Church is the community of those who respond to the call of God to repent – to centre their lives on God as revealed in Christ and not on selfish or any other lesser values. It is based on the prior grace of God. He is the sole source of its holiness. Its holiness does not mean it is perfect. It is essentially a mixed community of saints and sinners. Indeed the greatest saints are those who are most conscious of their sin. All Christians, those called to be saints, are in constant need of repentance, in a perpetual state of growth into maturity in Christ. Therefore the Church cannot be a sect of people who think themselves holier than others. Membership of the Church is marked by baptism, and the Church of England has always baptised infants.

The Church is Catholic
9. The Church of England has regarded itself as both Catholic

and Reformed. Because of its history, at times it expressed its faith polemically in contradistinction to that of Roman Catholicism on the one hand and Protestantism on the other. Because of its attempt to find a middle way it was often spoken of earlier in this century as a 'bridge Church', a place where Catholic and Protestant could meet and understand each other. Its comprehensive nature, however, is not that of a harmonious body in which all think alike. It is a body in which 'catholic', 'evangelical', 'liberal', 'radical' and 'charismatic' live side by side, accepting the same basic doctrine, authority and orders of ministry, but feeling free to interpret them differently and to lay emphasis on different aspects. Part of the difficulty Anglicans have found in searching for unity with other Churches has been that different groups in the Church are looking for unity in different directions and so the real value of the Church as a bridge is being questioned. An important element in the Church of England's programme is the search for a greater integration within it of groups with differing churchmanship.

The Church is Apostolic

10. From the time of the Reformation the Church of England regarded itself as the manifestation of the Catholic Church in England and it was at pains to preserve its continuity with the pre-Reformation Church, for example through maintaining the three-fold order of bishops, priests and deacons and through affirmation of the catholic creeds. This emphasis was reinforced by the Oxford Movement in the nineteenth century. Today there is much questioning about the role of the diaconate.

11. In recent years it has also begun to discover its apostolicity in terms of its missionary calling. From the end of the seventeenth century voluntary missionary associations have arisen to work overseas and at home. Overseas those societies are concerned to work in co-operation with other Churches, and not in competition with them. In England there is a gradual realisation that the Church of England's task can no longer be adequately fulfilled in pastoral terms, by expecting pastors to win back the lost sheep of our country. City parishes have become too populous and country parishes too geographically

extensive for this. More-over the cultural background of large sections of the population is no longer more than exiguously Christian, and some sections belong to other religions. In this context the exclusively Anglican, clerical, pastoral role has to be complemented by an ecumenical and missionary role, to be performed by ministers and laity working together.

Church, Nation and People

12.   The establishment of the Church of England has meant that it has a special relationship both with the English people and with the State. It enacts the religious rites of passage (at birth, marriage and death) for far more people than attend its regular worship. It marks the seasonal events of importance to groups in society, as at harvest festival. It also has a recognised place in the staging of religious ceremonies for the State (for example the Coronation and the Service of Thanksgiving following the conflict in the South Atlantic). Such ceremonies could become merely English civilisation at prayer. At their best, however, they witness to Jesus Christ and re-inforce Christian values in society.

13. The Church is by law established and has a particular responsibility to the nation and its political institutions. The traditional presence of certain bishops in the House of Lords gives an opportunity to the Church of England to contribute Christian and moral insights at the very point where law is made and government exercised.

14. This close link with the State also means that the Prime Minister advises the Queen on the appointment of bishops. In recent years an agreement has been adhered to whereby the Church presents two names, and the Prime Minister accepts or rejects one of them. Under this agreement the Prime Minister no longer exercises the right to nominate independently of the Church.

The Purpose of the Church

15. The Church of England attempts to fulfill its purpose in

worshipping, professing and proclaiming the faith and in bearing witness to Christian truth.

Worshipping

16. One of the motives of the Reformation in England was to translate the worship of the Church into the contemporary language of the people, and to give the congregation a fully responsive part in that worship. The Book of Common Prayer also contained more extensive Scripture readings than the liturgical books of any other Church. During this century there has been a renewed emphasis on the Eucharist as the central act of corporate worship every week, and a desire to celebrate baptism within corporate worship. In this way the Scriptures and the two sacraments of the Gospel are at the heart of worship, and corporate worship at the heart of the life of the Christian community.

17. As a result of the progress of the ecumenical movement, in 1972 the Church of England began to admit to communion communicant members of other Churches which subscribe to the doctrine of the Holy Trinity, and who are in good standing in their own Church.

The Church of England has never laid down rules for its own ordinary members about their receiving communion in other churches. This is left to individual conscience.

Canons are now being considered by the Church of England which would allow greater sharing in worship and ministry with other Churches.

Professing and proclaiming the faith

18. The Church believes in and announces to the world God's saving action in Jesus Christ crucified, risen and expected to come at the end of the world. The Jesus it proclaims is the Jesus who himself came announcing the Kingdom or rule of God. Jesus' proclamation of the Kingdom was not the implementation of a particular social plan or programme. It was opening people's eyes to the fact that God was with them in a new way for grace and for judgment. The Church is therefore called both to tell the story of Jesus and to point to God's grace

and judgment in the world today. The Church of England has particular responsibility to speak of these things both to people and to government.

19. It does this through its leaders, through formal synodical statements and representation, and through the words and actions of its members.

Witnessing
20. The Church does not cease to exist outside its gatherings for worship and in synod. The effective witness of the Church to Jesus and to the coming of his Kingdom is expressed most effectively by the Spirit's presence with small groups of Christians and with individual members of the Church as they live and act and speak (and suffer) as Christian citizens in the fulfilment of their everyday, secular occupations. It is becoming increasingly clear that this aspect of Christian mission is of primary importance, and that lay people need one another's help and the help of the clergy in fulfilling it. It is also evident that this can best be fulfilled ecumenically.

Martin Reardon
Board of Mission & Unity
30th April 1986

Congregational Federation

Members: 10,000   *Ministers: 105*   *Churches: 293*

The Nature and Purpose of our Congregational Churches

(a) In relation to other Christian Denominations

Congregationalists tend to think they are the free-est of Free Church people. This is largely the mind of those who are voluntarily associated in the Congregational Federation. Each church is independent in that it has no overriding hierarchy or external authority. Its discipline lies in its effort to find the guidance of the Holy Spirit and to do the will of God as it is discerned by us for the company of believers in that place.

As Congregationalists we know this makes us very vulnerable. It is all too easy to think that what we want must be God's will. But the consensus of the Church Meeting has a salutary brake on the individualist.

Church Meeting is the governing body of the Church – that is: the assembly of those who, professing faith in Jesus Christ as Lord and Saviour and accepting the Congregational way of sharing responsibility for the local church as members join in the exciting pursuit of guidance of that church's organisation. Of course we are all as prone as other Christians to make mistakes, and perhaps more ready to admit it than we used to be!

Another change of attitude – easier for us to adopt than by some other traditions – is willingness to accept other ways of worship as being right for other people, even if we don't find those ways 'right' for ourselves.

A long memory can recall a fiercely judgmental attitude to other denominations. Now we say that these ways that are foreign to us, help fellow Christians to find their way to God.

They may travel such different routes, but they are obviously sincere and good people worshipping the same one God in Trinity. So most of us are happy to join in United Services that may be according to a tradition very different from our own. But, much as we appreciate other traditions and forms of churchmanship and their efficacy we would hate all to be rolled out alike.

One of our ministers used the illustration of the huge variety of fish in the sea but whatever is made into fish fingers is reduced to uniformity. "We don't want to be fish-fingers!" To quote the former Bishop of Taunton "Unity described by Paul is a harmony not a unison. Variety is not a problem to be overcome – it is a necessity. It is a glory, not a problem. Any approach to unity that neglects or overcomes that variety is a mistake!" And Edward Carpenter – Dean of Westminster, spoke of 'the cutting edge of the denominations.'

It seemed that the Churches Unity Commission foundered on this. It started off – avowedly seeking unity without uniformity. But its final scheme arrived at a demand for uniformity that would have created a further batch of non-conformers in several denominations, had it been implemented. The Lima Document is also busy emphasising all the likenesses rather than enjoying being exhilarated by the differences, so that it appears to be another plea for uniformity. In our Lent 'very-ecumenical' discussion group on "What on earth is the Church for?" we were able to discuss and pray as fellow Christians – also to tease one another a little about our differences. A very happy state to have been acheived! To laugh and pray with other Christians is a wonderfully welding process and a great springboard for working together.

(b) God's Mission to the World.

God's Mission to the World is the Church in action. There will always be some 'passengers' who want a 'sedentary' faith to fit their own taste and comfort; that will make no claims apart from an hour a week for worship, and a cushion against adversity. But the emphasis on 'the priesthood of all believers' has real meaning for most Congregationalists. In practice, it means that a lay person – man or woman – can be approved by Church Meeting to preside at the Communion Service. It means that the local church through the church meeting can issue a call to anyone it believes will fulfill God's will and purpose as their pastor and similarly can ask for, or accept the resignation of such a one.

The wider interpretation of this 'priestly' function lays the reponsibility for evangelism on everyone. This includes sharing in the work of a number of missionary societies through prayer and financial support, especially for the Council for World Mission in which we have a particular responsibility. It also emphasises the bearing of the Good News wherever we are and wherever we go.

Most of our people would say that political weakness is in no small measure due to the lack of the impact of religion on politics. Truthfulness and trust are so obviously lacking in national and international affairs, and the pursuit of peaceful and friendly relationships is not engaged in with Christian concern and inspiration, as we would wish it to be. 'Politics' is about people and how they live together and we think is in desperate need for more Christian politicians and we rejoice when the Archbishops of Canterbury and York and the Free Church Moderators unitedly 'interfere'! We share the social concern of the Archbishop of Canterbury's Commission document 'Faith in the Inner City', and while the Church of England may confess it is too middle class, we claim to have an active and vocal 'working class' element in many of our churches. The years of full employment and 'affluence' may have removed the phenomenon of the non-conformist central missions working in the poor areas of big cities; in these days of desperate unemployment a number of our churches are meeting needs in imaginative ways and because of the independence of the local church, they are free to do so 'without tarrying for anie'.

In the 1972 beginnings of the Churches Unity Commission (then dubbed 'Talks about Talks') one of the objectives was the acknowledgement of each others' Ministries. The failure to achieve this objective was because of the demand of some for the re-ordination of those Ministers not episcopally ordained. This barrier was never broken down.

There is a high standard of training in Biblical and Theological studies for Ministers wishing to be on the Congregational Federation Roll of Ministers. And evidence of the man or woman's calling is required when a Congregational Church, in its freedom, calls one to be its pastor who is not on the Roll of Ministers; the required standard of training has to be attained, before acceptance on the Roll is possible. The Ministry of the Word and Sacraments: basically, we believe that we are one in Christ, whatever differing outward expression of worship, liturgy and church government may seem best to express the mind of Christ for different people.

(c) International Relationships

The Congregational Federation is part of the International Congregational Fellowship. It also is building special relationships with the Congregational Churches of Samoa and Guyana. It has helped support a West Indian church worker linked with our Brixton Church and its Minister.

Rev Elsie D Chamberlain B.D.
21st April 1986

Council of African and Allied Churches

Members: 2,500   *Ministers: 60★*   *Churches: none owned*

★The majority of ministers are not paid for their services
Figures supplied by the Council of African and Allied Churches

The Nature and Purpose of our Council in Relation to other Christian Denominations

The Church is that institution, which affords proof of its utility and is found elevating the race, rousing the dormant understanding from material beliefs to the apprehension of spiritual ideas and the demonstration of divine knowledge, thereby casting out devils, or error, and healing the sick. The Church is the structure of Truth and Love.

In our tradition and experience, the Church is by nature and commandment an apostolic community which exists for the sake of announcing the Gospel to all nations and of making them disciples of Christ. The function of the Church as apostolic messenger to individuals is clear-cut, but emphasis upon it ought not to lead to the obscuring of its mission to social groups. The Gospel must be preached in different fashion when it is addressed to a nation from the way in which it is proclaimed to individuals or groups. It is important and imperative that the Church should discharge its apostolic responsibility by envisaging the needs of men in their societies as well as in their isolation before God.

The Council of African and Allied Churches pledged itself to maintain fraternal relationships with other Christian denominations and to foster ecumenical understanding with other Christian churches and communities in order to further the unity of the Church. In order to acheieve this goal, efforts have been made to get involved whenever possible with other denominations by individual member churches of the Council.

Our churches being autonomous branches of the One, Holy, Apostolic Church of God, are striving purposely to experience and secure ecumenical relationship with other Christian denominations, but at present, that purpose is frustrated. It is still but imperfectly successful in local manifestations which cannot as yet transcend their own limitations. Every Christian group, at its level, is the organisation of a common life by something which is at least supra-natural. Christianity says that this is Man responding, in his measure, to the Divine. None of the groups can provide personal life with its full expression. Group come into conflict with group. There are genuine clashes of interest, some of which seem to admit of no compromise. There are grievances and suspicions which separate groups from one another. Until they are solved, the possibility of genuine ecumenism is remote, and the unity, which is total commitment to each other in a corporate life in Christ, prayed for by our Lord and Saviour-Jesus Christ will continue to be a dream. There is no way of transcending this finitude unless the purpose informing all churches is the will and purpose of God. That is what the Christian religion offers. The Holy Spirit could redeem the Church from the bankruptcy of human statesmanship. It could lead men to trust one another through all differences of race, doctrine and traditions. Christ, says St. Paul, 'slew the enmity'. The Holy Spirit cleanses hearts from fears and supicions. It demolishes the walls of partition and throws down the barricades of privilege. It begins to draw men across all that divides them, and the apparent conflicts of cross-purpose, into a fellowship which is universal because it is centred in the loved of God.

The resurgence of ancient faiths and cultures, and the world of religious pluralism in which we live, and the knowledge of great mass of mankind living outside in the streets, and the housing blocks where something is happening to which we must make some kind of response, and all other world situations, challenge us to dialogue and participate with others in building up a secular religious community which is concerned with man's common humanity alone.

Jesus saw, once for all, the urgent need for re-ordering human priorities. The older, which replaces God with the gods of this world, must radically change so that God takes His rightful place in His creation and man is liberated from the domination of the powers and principalities of this world. When this happens through the gift of God's grace, man becomes responsible for the world. The grace he receives from God becomes his commission, his privilege becomes his responsibility.

Jesus stands as the one who is responsible to God Alone. He invites us to transcend the piety and absolutism of the world, to hear afresh the voice of God, and to receive the gift of life within the matrix of faith, and give it back to the world. We need love to identify ourselves with the common humanity in these times where everything seems alien. The world requires us to affirm our identification and our common humanity in a new spirituality, even in the way you look at people. There is no time for long introductions. We need to learn to so look at people and to so respond to people that we do it from our common humanity and respond to the God Who is present in the Christ whom we meet in others. There is the way by which we can share in God's mission to the world.

Can we discern in these development (I mean the Inter Church Process), the Spirit of God leading us to a new understanding of God's way of working with man? To be in mission is to accept risks; to witness to the word of God is always hazardous. The truth we have received constitutes a danger, and the gift we have to share is a personal risk and responsibility. This close inter-connection between grace and commission, privilege and responsibility, giving up and receiving, losing and finding, serving and being served is crucial in Jesus' thinking about the world dominated by its piety and the kingdom of God which ends this domination through faith.

For the renewal of the Church and the fulfillment of her mission to the world, what we need is not more worship, more education, more buildings. To be sure, these are needed but they cannot be the priorities of a people engaged in mission of the world. What is urgently needed is the acceptance of one another, more risk-taking, more faith, more action, more people open to the world and living their lives for the life of others.

The Council of African and Allied Churches will endeavour ceaselessly to co-operate with other churches and denominations in the fulfillment of the commission to 'go and teach all nations, baptising then in the name of the Father, and of the Son, and of the Holy Ghost', and the realisation of the One Church of God.

His Grace, The Most Revd. Father Olu. A. Abiola
Chairman, Council of African and Allied Churches.

Independent Methodist Churches

Members: 4,300 *Ministers: 135* *Churches: 115*

1. Nature of the Church

The Independent Methodist Connexion's Statement of Faith (1984) defines its view of the Church in these terms:

> **"We believe that the Church is the whole compnay of the redeemed in heaven and on earth and consists of all who are united to God through faith in Christ. The Lord Jesus Christ is the head of the Church which is His Body."**

This definition contains several assertions which reflect the denomination's understanding of the Church.

(A) It pictures the Church globally, not confined within denominational boundaries, but embracing all who share a common faith in Christ. What this faith means is outlined more specifically in other sections of the Statement which deal with Christology and Soteriology (see Appendix). The standpoint which the denomination takes in relation to churches of other Communions is, therefore, one which recognises a spiritual oneness with all who acknowledge and trust the same Saviour and Lord.

(B) It is only right to point out that not all Independent Methodists see the need for spiritual unity to be translated into organis forms of union. The denomination has not taken any significant step towards union with any other church body and has, on the whole, shown a general reluctance to do so. It has not, for instance, covenanted for union as others in the United Kingdom have done. However, relationships with other churches both nationally and locally through various inter-church groups are generally very cordial and have often resulted in shared activities and ventures which have been mutually beneficial to the parties concerned.

(C) The assertion that the Lord Jesus Christ is the Head of the Church does more than make a routine statement of Scriptural truth. It emphasises the belief that no human leader can acceptably be described as Head of the Church even in a titular or figurative sense. Therefore, it has implications for the issue of leadership in the Church both locally and nationally.

(D) Central leadership in the Connexion of Independent Methodist Churches is the result of a collective decision-making process. There is a President who is appointed annually; in practice few Presidents serve for more than one year. The office, therefore, has no permanence though the President's leadership is honoured and respected and his oversight of the churches in a guiding and advisory capacity is greatly valued. However, any kind of oversight resembling a monarchical episcopate is not accepted, nor is it likely that it will be considered acceptable in the foreseeable future.

(E) Various patterns of leadership operate in local churches and the degree of authority exercised by leaders differd according to the standpoint of the individual church on this issue. Some churches have Connexionally recognised ministers who operate in a non-stipendiary capacity to fulfil the church's pastoral and preaching ministries; others are led by a President and others still by elders. In almost every case the leaders concerned are unpaid.

(F) This diverse pattern of leadership presents one of the most significant obstacles to inter-church relationships, since other denominations (the larger ones in particular) often show an unwillingness to recognise Independent Methodist ministers or other leaders as having a ministry of equal validity to their own. This has frequently been an obstacle to shared work and mission. The reasons for it are various and should be seen from the viewpoints of both the Independent Methodists themselves and the other churches concerned. The main problem appears to centre around the Independent Methodist tradition of receiving ministers at a service of 'recognition' rather than ordination. This form of service interprets ordination as something which is done by God alone and that the responsibility of the church is to 'recognise' the candidate who has, in the Church's view, been ordained by God for ministry. The laying on of hands has not, traditionally, been included in the service for this reason. However, thinking on this issue is not as uniform or rigid as it may have been a generation ago, as is evidenced by a recent conference which considered the issues raised in 'Baptism, Eucharist and Ministry'. This conference, consisting of a cross-section of people in the denomination, including several of its leading figures, took a very positive view of the appropriateness of the laying on of hands though it was not seen as being solely for the purpose of ordaining people to a single form of ministry. The conference also felt that 'commissioning' was a more fitting term than 'ordination'.

(G) Perhaps the most significant factor which governs inter-church relationships is that of the autonomy of the local church. The Independent Methodist Connexion is a body which consists of independent churches, all, of which own their own property and deeds, and none of which can be obliged to take any given course of action without its direct consent. This leads to the second major point about the Independent Methodist understanding of the nature of the church, namely the fact that each local church, in its own right, is an entity directly accountable to God for its life and mission. In practice, individual churches are often influenced, supported and sometimes guided by the Connexion which seeks to develop a common sense of direction on the part of all the churches which are within its constituency. Isolationism is discouraged, as churches are urged to be part of what God is doing through the denomination as a whole, the churches locally and the churches nationally.

2. Purpose of the Church

Again, the Statement of Faith gives the Connexion's definition of the Church's purpose:

"The purpose of the Church is to worship God, to promote the fellowship of His people, to preach the gospel and to make disciples of all nations".

(A) This fourfold definition of the church's purpose has major implications for the denomination's relationship with other churches and the question of a common mission to the world. Clearly, its links with our churches are only going to be effective where there is a shared commitment to the great commission and to the creation of a Christ-centred community in which faith is genuinely shared and expressed by all members. The churches which comprise the denomination were born through an evangelistic process and, despite subsequent theological changes which led to an emphasis on social and moral issues rather than evangelism, there is currently a tendency to return to a more clearly-defined evangelical base.

Consequently, there is a readiness on the part of many to be involved with fellow-Christians of other denominations in evangelistic work (e.g. in Mission England).

(B) The readiness to work with Christians of various backgrounds is nowhere better illustrated than in the field of Overseas Missions work. There is no denominational missionary society so that members who are called to overseas work fulfil their calling through various interdenominational societies. This position is not the result of the denomination's inability to maintain a missionary society (though it would be difficult for a small denomination to do so.) It is simply felt to be undesirable to export British denominationalism overseas and that missionary work should lead to the formation of churches which are truly indigenous to the countries in which they are established.

(C) Whilst Social Responsibility is fully accepted as part of the ministry of the church, it can never be a substitute for the proclamation of the gospel of the saving work of the Lord Jesus Christ. This is the mission which the Lord Himself gave to His Church and it claims priority over every other aspect of the church's programme and lifestyle.

(D) The function of the church as a means of fellowship for God's people need not be interpreted merely in the sense of the individual church providing fellowship for its own members. Gatherings of Christians from a variety of churches for purposes of worship, prayer, learning and service are all valid expressions of the fellowship life of the Church. Independent Methodists tend to be very willing to be involved in this kind of sharing.

(E) The promotion of a Christian lifestyle on the part of every member is very much part of the purpose of Independent Methodist Churches. The absence of a separated clergy tends to elevate the importance of the individual member. The Statement of Faith affirms:

> **"We believe in the priesthood of all believers, affirming that each believer has direct access to God through the Lord Jesus Christ. The individual is required to render obedience to Christ in every area of life, seeking always, under his direction, the advancement of His Kingdom."**

The practical operating of the individual churches depends very much on the application of this principle and it is seen as part of the church's purpose to develop a life of discipleship on the part of its members.

Appendix

STATEMENT OF FAITH

1. The Trinity
We believe in One Living and True God, Creator of all, eternal in three persons as Father, Son and Holy Spirit; Him alone we worship and adore.

2. God The Father
We believe that God the Father Almighty, in holy love, gave his Son for the salavation of mankind.

3. God The Son
We believe that the Lord Jesus Christ is God the Son. For our sake he became man, was truly human and truly divine, and lived a sinless human life.
We believe that He reveals the Father, that He died to atone for our sins, rose from the dead, ascended to Heaven and was exalted. He is our Advocate, Mediator and Lord.

We believe that He will return personally in power and glory.

4. God The Holy Spirit

We believe that God the Holy Spirit convinces of sin, righteousness and judgment. He causes those who repent to be born anew and dwells within them, witnessing to their salvation and developing the fruit of a Godly life. He endows believers with gifts for the upbuilding of the Church. He glorifies Jesus.

5. Mankind

We believe that all people are sinful and are unable to deliver themselves from the guilt, penalty and power of their sin.

6. Salvation

We believe that salvation from the guilt, penalty and power of sin to eternal life is a free gift of God.

Salvation is His purpose for all mankind and is only possible through personal faith in the atoning work of the Lord Jesus Christ.

We believe that all must stand before the final judgment of Christ and that those who have refused His salvation will be separated eternally from God.

7. The Bible

We believe that the Scripture of the Old and New Testaments are the inspired Word of God and are the supreme authority in all matters of faith and conduct.

8. The Church

We believe that the Church is the whole company of the redeemed in heaven and on earth and consists of all who are united to God through faith in Christ.

We believe that the Lord Jesus Christ is the head of the Church, which is His body. The purpose of the Church is to worship God, to promote the fellowship of His people, to preach the Gospel and to make disciples of all nations.

9. Sacraments

We believe that the sacraments of baptism and the Lord's Supper are to be practised in obedience to the command of the Lord Jesus Christ.

We believe that in the observance of the Lord's Supper Christ Himself is certainly and really present, though not bodily in the elements.

When used by believers with faith and prayer, the sacraments are through the operation of the Holy Spirit, outward and visible signs of inward and spiritual grace.

10. The Christian Life

We believe in the priesthood of all believers, affirming that each believer has direct access to God through the Lord Jesus Christ. The individual believer is required to render obedience to Christ in every area of life, seeking always, under His direction, the advancement of His Kingdom.

STATEMENT OF PRACTICE

1. Churches
Each Church is self-governing. Subject to the Church's trust deed, the members' meeting is the final authority in all matters affecting the Church.

2. Circuits
Groups of Churches are associated in Circuits for mutual benefit. The meetings of the Circuits are deliberative in character and recommendations can only be made effective by the co-operation of each Church. The organisation of each circuit is outlined in its rules.

3. Connexion
All member Churches constitute the Connexion of Independent Methodist Churches. The organisation of the Connexion is outlined in its constitution.

4. Ministries
(a) Every believer is called to service in the Kingdom of God, there being no distinction between one service and another beyond that of function. It is recognised that differing gifts and ministries are bestowed on believers for the benefit of the Church as a whole. Each Church should therefore, recognise and cultivate the gifts and ministries of its members.

(b) To assist pastoral responsibility and the wider ministry of the Word of God, the Connexion appoints as ministers of the denomination those, called by God and duly nominated by their Churches and Circuits, who have satisfied Connexional requirements of calling and training. Such ministers serve their Church, Circuit and the Connexion without remuneration.

(c) Provision may be made for the maintenance of those appointed to specific ministries, such as evangelists or missionaries.

5. Mission
The Connexion is concerned with the spread of the Gospel at home and overseas. Where required, Churches and Missions are assisted and new Churches or Missions may be formed, using Connexional resources of finance and personnel.

Methodist Church in Great Britain
(including the Synods of Scotland and Shetlands)

Members: 450,000★   *Ministers: 3,300*   *Churches: 7,700*

★ *Figure given by church*

A British Methodist Response

The Methodist Church has its origins in the ministry of John and Charles Wesley in the 18th century, and the circumstances, personalities and convictions of that period have left their mark upon our heritage. It has been customary to summarise Methodist emphases in a series of epigrammatic statements: "all people need salvation", "all people can be saved", "all can know they are saved", "all can be saved to the uttermost", "there is no such thing as solitary religion". We have tried to stand back from these traditional statements of our identity and look at ourselves afresh, but in doing so we have been conscious of the debt which the Methodist Church in Britain still owed to its past. We also recognize that a statement such as this cannot be purely descriptive but must to some extent reflect the ideal to which we strive to conform, for it would be impossible to include a reference to every local variation and difference of emphasis in a church of over 450,000 members.

We see the life of the church in terms of mission. Without attempting to deny the importance of understanding the church in terms of the people of God gathered for worship we are convinced that to neglect the mission of the church is to betray its fundamental responsibility. While Methodist churches are grouped in geographical units, known as circuits, we have never rigidly adhered to the model either of a parish or a gathered church. All churches maintain not only a list of members but in addition a community roll of those who have varying degrees of association with the church. We do not interpret the word "mission" in any narrow sense. John Wesley believed that God had raised up the Methodist people "to spread scriptural holiness throughout the land". He was as much concerned for the continued growth of individuals in godliness as for their initial awakening to saving faith, and as much concerned for godliness and justice in the life of the nation (and its dealings with the colonies) as with the conversion of individuals. We are still convinced that evangelism, care within the community and the struggle for justice must go hand in hand in the church's mission.

From the beginning Methodists were organised in small groups for mutual support and pastoral care exercised for one another. While many of the formal structures for this purpose familiar in eighteenth and nineteenth centuries have disappeared there is still a strong sense of belonging in Methodist congregations, which is expressed, not only in the welcome offered on arrival, and in conversation before and after worship, but also in the more formal requirement that every member's name be recorded and reviewed annually and a ticket of membership issued. There is a strong sense of nurture, evidenced in the expectation that young people, baptized in infancy, will be led in growing awareness through Sunday School, Junior Church and Family Worship to personal commitment to Christ, and so on to conformation, active participation in the church's life, and the holding of office where appropriate. There are very few churches (generally the very small) where activities are restricted to services of worship on a Sunday. In most churches one would expect to find a variety of midweek activities for different age groups and for different purposes which may range from the predominantly social to the predominantly devotional. These give opportunities for many to exercise gifts of leadership and to share responsibility through committee work for aspects of the common life.

People in practice associate themselves with the church and come to embrace Christian faith for a variety of reasons. While the language of "Christian experience" is sometimes carelessly used to give a false impression that Christian truth can only be validated by experience, Methodists generally would take it for granted that Christian belief should be a conviction consciously appropriated for oneself, deeply held and progressively effecting a transformation of attitudes and relationships. Brought about by the work of the Holy Spirit, such faith is a possibility for every one. The annual covenant service held throughout the Methodist Church at the beginning of January, in which God's saving work is celebrated and commitment is renewed, gives form expression to this sense of personal trust and dedication within the corporate setting of God's covenant with his people.

The covenant service also witnesses to an understanding of Christian discipleship in terms of growth which it is appropriate to review from time to time. We have already referred to the emphasis in our churches upon nurture in the life of the church. We have inherited a tradition of training and authorisation, not only for our ordained ministers, but for our lay preachers, workers with children, young people and others. Training is required of those who hold such offices. One of the roots of this tradition is John Wesley's own appeal to reason, along with Scripture, tradition and experience, in discovering the will of God. More widely, meetings for study, prayer and mutual support are once more becoming common in our churches. While few Methodist would nowadays use the traditional language of "holiness" or "perfect love", such meetings are evidence of a continuing conviction that Christian discipleship involves a life in the Spirit which is to be fostered.

While an historian would probably agree that the political sympathies of the majority of Methodists have changed over the years, we have inherited from the 18th century a conviction about the social outworkings of the gospel which expressed itself, for example, in Wesley's support of the campaign to abolish slavery, or 100 years later in the strong backing given to the temperance movement, in the building of our central missions with their programmes of relief for the disadvantaged, and more recently, in the development of our Division of Social Responsibility which is charged with the preparation of statements on social and political issues on behalf of the church. The National Children's Home and Methodist Homes for the Aged are charities on a national scale, but are an integral part of the organization of the church. Since 1984 we have been raising a fund of one million pounds for Mission Alongside the Poor in urban and rural areas and have been able to support nearly 70, mostly small scale, projects organised by Methodists as a result of local initiatives. While the majority of Methodists would not advocate radical political change we share a strong conviction that Christian faith must express itself in activity to relieve suffering and secure justice. Many local churches are involved in community projects of various kinds, such as playgroups, clubs for the elderly, projects for the unemployed.

Worship in the Methodist Church owes something to both the Anglican and the Free Church traditions. There is a high expectation of preaching as a means by which faith is shared, and commitment generated, and a medium through which the living God is encountered. We are heirs of the Protestant Reformation in giving primacy to Scripture in our doctrinal standards, and this is reflected in our worship and in the training of preachers, lay and ordained. Methodism practises the baptism of infants, believing this to be a sacramental proclamation of prevenient grace. Holy Communion is celebrated in most Methodist churches at least once a month, and there has been a growing emphasis upon its importance as we have progressively recovered a sense of the place it occupied in early Methodism and of the contribution Charles Wesley made to eucharistic devotion through his hymns. Hymnody is in fact the key to our tradition of worship. The Methodist Hymn Book and its successor Hymns and Psalms, authorised for use by the Methodist Conference, are akin in their importance to the Prayer Book for Anglicans. They enshrine and communicate our theology and spiritually and are perhaps the strongest element in our common identity, for their use is virtually universal. Also important is the Methodist Service Book, last revised in 1975, which, while not obligatory, is widely used for baptism, confirmation, holy communion and some other services, and contributes to the common character of our worship. The lectionary of the Joint Liturgical Group, incorporated in the Service Book, is increasingly used.

While many Methodists are hardly aware of more than their

local church, in fact each congregation is part of a national structure embracing England, Scotland, Wales, Shetland, the Isle of Man and the Channel Islands, under the ultimate authority of the Methodist Conference, and regulated by a common form of church order. The standing orders of the Conference, incorporated in the Constitutional Practice and Discipline, and periodically revised, regulate administration in every sphere of the church's life, local and national. Pastoral oversight, exercised by many, ordained and lay, in diverse forms of ministry, ultimately resides in the oversight (*episcope*) of the Conference. This is not a matter of concern only to those with an interest in theological or constitutional questions. It is a matter of experience, for example, for young people who are enabled to share in activities at regional and national level through the Methodist Association of Youth Clubs. The most obvious expression of this "connexional" character is the ordained ministry. Ministers are generally appointed, not to a single local church (68% of the 7,500 local churches have less than 60 members), but to a circuit or local group of churches, which is the primary administrative unit, and in the last analysis are stationed there by act of the Conference, although in practice many appointments are made by mutual agreement between the minister and the circuit. Ministerial appointments to circuits are for a minimum of five years, and in practice longer periods are becoming common, but the expectation is that every minister will move to a new appointment regularly, and this reinforces the sense that the ordained ministry is shared with the whole church. The sense of belonging to a single body, with uniform status and virtual equality of stipend, is strong among ministers, all of whom are subject to a common discipline through the Conference, and thus are answerable to one another. While some ministers, appointed as chairmen of districts, fulfill many duties which can properly be described as episcopal, and relate to episcopal colleagues in other churches, there are no bishops in British Methodism. Their appointment as chairmen is not for life, and they may in due course return to a circuit appointment again.

There are other aspects to our 'connexional character': members are members of the whole church and are transferred when they remove from one locality to another; a system of grant support, and (in property matters) report and building consent, ensures that the strong can help the weak and that wider resources and experience can be made available to the smallest congregation. If it is sometimes observed by others that Methodists seek each other out and in that sense form a sub-culture, this is because there is a discernible common character to Methodist churches throughout Great Britain. It is an important fact of our history that, although there were numerous divisions in the 19th century, we have not had the tradition of defined theological parties in the church. Today various traditions, liberal, conservative, charismatic, radical, find their place within a common pattern of life. A wider aspect of this national bonding, which links with what was said above about mission, is the fact that the Methodist Missionary Society, officially the Overseas Division of the Methodist Church, is an integral part of the church, and every church member is automatically a member of it. Its 1985/6 budget amounts to £3.8 million. Mission in a world context is not an optional extra for Methodists, and recently steps have been taken to bring this home by arranging for ministers and lay people from other areas of the world to serve in churches in Britain. We are members of the World Methodist Council which brings together churches with an approximate member-ship of 23 millions for a variety of shared enterprises, including ecumenical bilateral dialogue, theological study, and evangelism.

Methodist ministers, men and women, married and single, are ordained by prayer with the laying on of hands by ministers previously so ordained, at a service held by authority of the Conference. The President of the Conference, or his deputy, presides. Ordination is preceded by a period of training, in most cases residential, but also including a probationary period in a circuit appointment. To be accepted as a candidate for training one must first have qualified as a lay preacher. The ordained ministry is seen within the context of the ministry entrusted by Christ to all God's people, for every member of the church has a contribution to make to ministry in worship, service and witness in the world, although Methodism can offer its own examples of acquiescence in ministerial domination. It is symbolic of this emphasis upon lay ministry that the two senior officers and national representatives of the church, elected annually, the President and Vice-President of the Conference, respectively a minister and a lay person, and among the latter, five of the last ten have been women. Women in fact play a major part in the life of the Methodist church, frequently in positions of responsibility in the local church and circuit, less often at district or regional level, or in the committees of the church.

"The Methodist Church claims and cherishes its place in the Holy Catholic Church which is the Body of Christ" (Deed of Union, para 30). We have written of ourselves because we were invited to do so but without wishing to make exclusive claims or to belittle what God has given to others. We welcome the opportunity to be open to Christians of other denominations. We have received much from the ecumenical movement in this century, have given our agreement to two sets of proposals for union in England, and have gladly consented to the participation of daughter churches in unions in India, Zambia and elswhere. We are involved in more than 330 Local Ecumenical Projects. Three of our four centres for residential training of ordained ministers are ecumenical. John Wesley was remarkable for his openess to Christians of other communions, trying always to go behind the 'opinions' which caused divisions to the 'heart', the shared loyalty to Christ. This was for him the 'catholic spirit'. So our catholicity tends to look for common ground with others before attending to our differences, although, along with Christians of other traditions we find it easier to work and worship with those who are 'like us', and recognize that there are many barriers of misunderstanding still to be broken down.

Along with other churches we are now more diverse than at any time in our history, and what we have written above may seem over-optimistic in the light of the theological and social pluralism of the 1980s. But we are surprised how often our traditional values reassert themselves in new forms. There are signs of renewal in the life of the church and readiness to respond to the call of God to mission in new ways. We have referred above to Mission Alongside the Poor. The Methodist Association of Youth Clubs, now 40 years old, continues to be one of the largest national youth organisations gathering 12,000 young people in London for the annual weekend. Luton Industrial College has sought for 30 years to serve the church in mission to industrial society and to stimulate serious study of the issues involved. We have recently appointed an officer for community and race relations. We adopted in 1985 new procedures for stationing ministers which are intended to make a more flexible response to the needs of mission. We have been stimulating more imaginative use of the gifts of lay people in various forms of ministry. We have a long tradition of the use of lay men and women in pastoral and preaching as well as administrative roles in the church, and have been trying to ensure that these avenues of service did not become stereotyped. A recent report, **Sharing in God's Mission**, now being widely studied, seeks to encourage every congregation and circuit to develop a policy for mission and to plan the use of resources to that end. We have been making serious attempts to rationalise our use of buildings and adapt them for contemporary conditions of worship and community service.

In 1988 the Methodist Church will celebrate the 250th anniversary of the conversion of John Wesley in Aldersgate Street, London in 1738. It will be an opportunity for celebration, and for study and reflection on the meaning of his experience for the church in the late 20th century. We shall be joined in this by representatives of Methodist churches in other parts of the world. We shall invite our fellow Christians to share the occasion with us. We want to learn from the past, but not be bound by it, to be open to the future, but not in isolation. We hope that **Not Strangers But Pilgrims** may help us to be more aware of what God has given to each Christian communion, what we can share with one another, and how bridges can be built, so that Christ's mission to the world may be more faithfully continued through us all.

Moravian Church in Great Britain and Ireland

Members: 3,700   *Ministers: 34*   *Churches: 43*

The present day Moravian Church is descended from the *Unitas Fratrum* (Unity of the Brethren) which came into being in Bohemia in 1457, among a radical group of the followers of the reformer John Hus. In the eighteenth century, following a long period of persecution in its homeland when it continued only as an underground movement, The church was renewed at Herrnhut in Saxony by religious refugees from Bohemia and Moravia.

At that time, elements from the thought and practice of the old Unity were confirmed in the life of the renewed Church and new elements were introduced, springing from the creative religious genius as well as the Lutheran background of Count Zinzendorf, on whose estate the Czech refugees found shelter and who became a leader of the renewed Church.

Among these elements were the following, which have continued to influence the thought and practice of the Moravian Church up to the present.

1. An acceptance of the threefold ministry of deacons, presbyters and bishops. The bishop ordains and gives spiritual leadership to the Church but does not have administrative authority by virtue of office.

While this is the pattern Moravians have accepted as right for their own ministry, they do not believe that episcopacy is of the essence of the Church, nor that episcopal ordination is essential for a valid ministry. They have no difficulty therefore in working in the closest union with Churches whose understanding of ministry is different from theirs. They hold strongly to the doctrine of the priesthood of all believers.

2. A recognition of the Bible as the ultimate source and rule of faith, doctrine and life for the Unitas Fratrum.

In addition to this, the Church has recognised the value of a number of traditional credal statements in helping the Church to formulate its thought but believes that the mystery of Jesus Christ cannot be comprehended completely by any human statement.

Those entering the Church, therefore, are not required to give formal assent to any creed or doctrinal statement beyond an acknowledgement of Jesus Christ as Saviour and Lord. Members of the Moravian Church are allowed a great deal of personal freedom in interpreting and understanding the Christian Faith. "In essentials, unity; in non-essentials, liberty; in all things, charity" sums up the Moravian attitude both to doctrine and practice.

3. A special emphasis on the Christian Church as a fellowship of believers.

This is a particular emphasis within our own denomination to the extent that the world Moravian Church is known as 'The Unity'. It leads on to a concern for the growing unity of the whole Christian Church.

"It is the Lord's will that Christendom should give evidence of and seek unity in him with zeal and love. In our own midst we see how such unity has been laid upon us as a charge. We recognise that through the grace of Christ the different churches have received many gifts. It is our desire that we may learn from each other and rejoice together in the riches of the love of Christ and the manifold wisdom of God.

We confess our share in the guilt which is manifest in the severed and divided state of Christendom. By means of such divisions we ourselves hinder the message and the power of the gospel. We recognise the danger of self-righteousness and judging others without love.

Since we together with all Christendom are pilgrims on the way to meet our coming Lord, we welcome every step that brings us nearer the goal of unity in him. He himself invites us to communion in his supper. Through it he leads the Church towards that union which he has promised. By means of his presence in the Holy Communion he makes our unity in him evident and certain even today."*

On the basis of such thinking, it is natural that the worship of the Moravian Church, including the Holy Communion, should be open to all who wish to share in it. In the same way, Moravians have no difficulty in accepting other forms of Christian worship as valid responses to the gospel.

4. This ecumenical emphasis led the eighteenth century Moravians to the belief that they were called by God to mission to the world, but not to plant Moravian congregations in areas where there were already well established churches. In continental Europe and in Britain there was extreme reluctance to organise separate Moravian congregations. Moravians worked in co-operation with Lutherans in Europe and with Anglicans in Britain, often directing their converts back to the local Parish Church. Something of this attitude has continued, for good or bad, through the years, with the result that the Church has remained very small in Europe and Britain. It was sustained however as a separate denomination by the conviction that it was called to mission to the world in areas where the gospel had not been preached and by seeing itself as part of the international Church that came into being as a result of that mission.

5. This vocation to mission has further led the Moravian Church to see itself as a community of service. There has always been a much greater interest in the working out of the meaning of the gospel in service than in working out its meaning in doctrinal statements.

"Jesus Christ came not to be served but to serve. From this, the Church received its mission and its power for service, to which each of its members is called. We believe that the Lord has called us particularly to mission service among the peoples of the world. In this and in all other forms of service.....he expects us to confess him and witness to his love in un-selfish service.

Jesus Christ maintains in love and faithfulness his commitment to this fallen world. Therefore we must remain concerned for this world. We may not withdraw from it through indifference, pride or fear. Together with the universal Christian Church, the Unitas Fratrum challenges mankind with the message of the love of God, striving to promote the peace of the world and to attain what is best for all men."*

From what has been written above, it will be clear that the Moravian Church in no way regards itself as having some unique truth that others do not have, either in its doctrine or its practice. We do believe that the particular emphases we make, the particular combination of elements of Christian thought and practice that has developed and the concern for freedom under Christ reflect aspects of Christian truth that are worth preserving in any moves towards fuller Christian unity. We are happy to share our thinking with the wider Church through this paper.

* *Quotations are from "Church Order of the Unitas Fratrum, 1981".*

Old Baptist Union

Members: 800　　　*Ministers: 22*　　　*Churches: 20*

The Old Baptist Union comprises a small group of Baptist churches formed in 1880.

Its Statement of Faith is based on two of the earliest Baptist confessions dated 1611 and 1660. From its inception the ethos of the Union has been wholly evangelical. The earlier 'aggressive' evangelistic activity showing some similarity to the present-day charismatic movement eventually gave way to a strong conservative evangelicalism and an understanding of the church as the 'gathered' church. The following statements from the Articles of Faith will give some indications not only of the doctrinal position but also the 'flavour' of its churchmanship over the past 100 years.

> We believe in the full inspiration of the Bible, accepting it as the Word of God, and regarding its teaching as of supreme and final authority in all matters of faith and practice.

> We believe that, by His grace, and through the merits of Jesus Christ, God has made full provision for the salvation of all men, but that those only will be saved who repent of their sins, and accept Christ, by faith, as their Saviour.

> We believe in Christ's death upon the Cross as an atoning sacrifice for sin; we believe in His bodily Resurrection; in His Ascension into Heaven, there to "appear in the presence of God for us", and in His personal Coming Again to receive His people to Himself, and to establish His Millennial Kingdom.

> We believe in the Personality and Deity of the Holy Spirit, and in His continued presence in the Church; and that His gifts may still be claimed and exercised, subject to His will.

We believe in the need of obedience to "all things whatsoever" Christ has commanded; and that the way of obedience is the way of sanctification, power and blessing.

This uncompromising evangelical doctrine and understanding of the church resulted in a staunch refusal to fellowship with churches having another view, either of authority or the way of salvation. Not just because it was felt that such fellowship would compromise the clear Gospel witness but rather due to the belief that fellowship in any meaningful sense was an impossibility.

Traditionally there has been a strong aversion to the 'social' Gospel. The emphasis being that the primary service of the church is to proclaim the Gospel of saving grace to lost mankind. Although this priority is still firmly established there has been a deeper understanding in recent years of the 'whole' Gospel related not only to personal salvation but to justice in society. This in turn has meant a greater willingness to listen to and co-operate with others whose emphases may be different.

To summarise, the Union is and always has been evangelical and has tended to fellowship and co-operate only with fellow evangelicals in other denominations. Whilst the evangelical emphasis remains there has emerged in the past twenty years a desire to understand the insights and contributions of other sections of the church. This desire has been expressed by local churches through membership of the British Council of Churches and the Free Church Federal Council. Several churches have participated recently in local ecumenical projects and have been involved in the Lent Study Course entitled **'What on Earth is the Church For?'**

Few members of the Old Baptist Union would feel that one United Church in Britain is either feasible or desirable, but there is a growing respect for other communions and a real desire to build bridges through prayer and debate towards a mutual understanding.

Religious Society of Friends (Quakers)

Members: 18,000★   *Ministers: –*   *Churches: 455*

★ *Figure given by church*

The Religious Society of friends (Quakers) in Great Britain (London Yearly Meeting) comprises some 18,000 members. Even adding the very many attenders who enrich the life of our meetings it is a very small body in relation to many of the other churches taking part in the Inter-Church process. London Yearly Meeting is the final constitutional authority of Friends in Great Britain. It is one of over fifty autonomous Yearly Meetings, with a total membership of some 200,000, which make up the Society of Friends world-wide.

Friends in Great Britain meet for worship and to conduct church affairs at the local (preparative meeting), area (monthly meeting), regional (general meeting), and national (Yearly Meeting) level. All rely equally for their authority and effectiveness on the presence and guidance of the Holy Spirit. The nature of our church therefore is neither congregational nor centralised, but a structure of widening groups through which our dependence on the Spirit can be tested and deepened. Our history is relatively short. Nevertheless we value our traditions and our Yearly Meeting's **Book of Christian discipline**, which is revised in every generation, aims to capture the essence of our spiritual experience and to related it to contemporary needs.

Amid the religious ferment of mid seventeenth-century England, George Fox (1624–91) became disillusioned with the standards of the church of his day and came after some struggle to a personal experience of Christ. Drawing on both Puritan and Anabaptist elements Fox taught that the visible church had fallen away from its apostolic roots and that Christ had now come to gather the true church. His message aroused a ready response among existing sectarian groups, particularly Independents and Seekers. A series of meetings in Lancashire and Westmorland in 1652 made of Quakerism a significant movement, which spread rapidly to the rest of England and to Europe and North America. In Robert Barclay (1648-90) it found its systematic theologian whose **Apology for the True Christian Divinity** used Scripture and the Church Fathers to support the distinctive Quaker insights as the central truths of New Testament Christianity.

In the eighteenth century however Quakerism lost its missionary zeal, with Friends accepting their status as a 'peculiar people'. The Quietest teaching they adopted stressed the worthlessness of human qualities of intellect and reason when set against the divine leadings of the Spirit. Quakerism today still exhibits the strains of this withdrawal from a potentially universal movement to a distinctive and limited sect, and there are groups in the Society today which seek to recapture the wider scope and activity of the seventeenth-century movement.

The evangelical movement in the nineteenth century brought Friends out of their isolation into a wide variety of work with their fellow-Christians. It also led to some doctrinal narrowness. By the end of the century, however, Friends had in large measure come to terms with the new scientific and biblical thought of the day. Rifts in American Quakerism, missionary endeavour, and the spread of Quakerism in Asia, Africa and South America have led to a great diversity of conviction and practice. While it is easy to speak of the richness of unity in diversity it is not nearly as easy to face and to try to grapple with it in practice.

The Church exists, we believe, to lead men and women, members and non-members alike, to a closer communion with God and to carry out those tasks which the Spirit lays upon it, to further the coming of God's kingdom on earth. We would wish to be seen as part of the church which is engaged in that process. We would no longer insist, with George Fox, that Quakerism represents the restored apostolic church and that all other churches are 'in the fall'. Our strong belief in the continuing revelation of the Holy Spirit would rather suggest that all the churches are still in the process of fulfilling God's purposes for them, and that Quakerism is no exception. It is also true to say that Quakers are less concerned with defining the church visible than recognising the priority of the church invisible, whose bounds are known only to God.

At the same time though, as we acknowledge our failures and imperfections, we assert, both from our tradition and our present experience, that lives which display the fruits of the Spirit have been nurtured within the Society of Friends. Without ordained clergy, liturgy and outward sacraments, we find that God, present in our meetings and in our hearts, enables us by grace to follow the path of discipleship of Jesus. We gratefully acknowledge that the faithful witness of God's people, in all the diverse branches of the Church, forms a tradition in which we seek to play our part.

It seems to us that each part of the Church rightly witnesses to certain testimonies, which it perceives particularly clearly and which it holds in trust for the rest. The distinctive insights of the Society of Friends derive from our sense of the direct, unmediated presence of God, which is available to each individual and to each gathered group.

This leads us to assert that sacramental practices are not in our experience necessary for the operation of God's grace. Our understanding of baptism is that it is not a single act of initiation but a continuing growth in the Holy Spirit and a commitment which must continually be renewed. We acknowledge that the grace of God is experienced by many through the outward rite of water-baptism, but for us there is no necessary connection between this single event in a person's life, and the experience of transformation by the Spirit. We cannot see that this rite should be used as the only way of becoming a member of the body of Christ; for us membership of the Society of Friends is a public acknowledgement of a growing unity with a community of people whose worship and service reflect, however imperfectly, their perception of Christian discipleship.

In Quaker worship neither the elements of bread and wine nor any other eucharistic liturgy is used. We meet in silence and wait on God for the words that may come, to any of us, from the depths of that waiting together. It is our experience that the reality of God's presence is not restricted to any particular eucharistic form and that it may be fully known in worship that retains none of the traditional elements that are central to the life of many churches. We recognise from the experience of our meetings for worship many of the spiritual aspirations expressed in the symbolism of the eucharist. We too see worship as the means of communion between the human and the divine, celebrating the work of God in creation, renewing and binding together the members of the worshipping body. We interpret the words and actions of Jesus as an invitation to recall and re-enact the self-giving nature of God's love at every meal and every meeting with others, and to allow our own lives to be broken open and poured out for the life of the world.

Our conviction that our only authority is the power of God, acting through the individual discipline and the gathered meeting, has also led us to different patterns of church life. We see our meetings for church affairs as meetings for worship for business, in which ideally the sacred and secular are woven into one. In an expectant waiting under the headship of Christ Friends have sought God's purposes, an experience which makes the practice of voting an irrelevance and which can lead to a sense of unity which far outweighs that of any human consensus. We recognise the gifts of the Spirit in leadership and ministry, but for us the gifts attach rather to the task than to the person and, though we have no separated ordained ministry, in one lifetime a person may be called to a number of different ministries. Such a call may come equally to a man or a woman; the Spirit has led us from our foundation to recognise the equality of women and men in the people of God. It is clear to us that authority in the Church can only be authentic as it conforms to the model of Christ, and that the priestly task of exercising Christ's functions in the world belongs to the whole community of God.

One of our distinctive testimonies, a sense that religious experience cannot be defined in credal formulae, and a consequent reluctance to be bound by them, has kept London Yearly Meeting from membership of the World Council of Churches and from full membership of the British Council of

Churches. Despite this, London Yearly Meeting has played a full part in the ecumenical movement from the 1910 World Missionary Conference onwards, and the recent exercise of responding to **Baptism, Eucharist and Ministry** has shown the continuing commitment at all levels of the Society to deepening our understanding of our relationships with our Christian churches. However this exercise also revealed fears lest **BEM** should be but one more step to equate 'visible unity' with 'organic unity', and in this Friends were echoing a position which London Yearly Meeting has maintained consistently since 1916, that the basis of Christian unity can never lie in agreement on doctrine and practice since it already exists in our common response to the demands of Christ. Hence, though we remain sympathetic to the pain of those branches of the Church who are struggling to draw closer to each other, especially in their understanding of their sacraments and ordained ministries, we are unable to share their sense of sin and guilt.

There are those in our membership who are ill at ease with orthodox formulations of Christian belief and doctrine, but are nevertheless demonstrably among those who do the will of God. There are also those who are concerned that the unique claims of Christianity render its position suspect in any attempt at dialogue with the other great world religions. This group would suggest that early Friends' stress on the universatility of the Spirit frees Quakers from this problem and gives them a useful role in such dialogue. We are aware of the need to represent this group among our membership, and perhaps among the membership of other churches, and all Quakers would wish to align themselves with those of other faiths, as well as with other Christians, who are working for reconciliation and healing in a broken world.

We are more likely to experience our sense of sin and guilt in our failure to live up to the demands of Christ in the world. To us, no separation between faith and practice can be valid. As the evils of modern society become daily more apparent, it is essential, if our mission and service is to be effective, for it to be deeply grounded in the life of the worshipping community and the personal response of the individual. This was the foundation for the historic work for social justice – prison reform, anti-slavery, war-time relief – which has given today's Society of Friends such a reputation to live up to. Similar work continues in the Society today, as in all the churches, as we wrestle with the problems of unemployment and the inner cities. It has been our conviction for over 300 years that the teaching of Jesus Christ forbids all participation in war. We are still exploring the implications of this testimony. There is a witness for God in the heart of our enemy, a truth which the nuclear threat makes it more urgent to proclaim. We have been involved most recently in testing the law on non-payment of the proportion of personal taxation which goes towards defence expenditure. We are becoming more aware of how our peace testimony involves our testimony to social justice and underpins all our social activities. It is a testimony which must be witnessed to on every level of modern life, from international diplomacy to personal reconciliations, and which makes strenuous demands on every one of us.

When the Inter-Church Process was first broached, we expressed our reservations about 'a further exercise of doctrinal debate when the world around us is in need of action on issues of poverty, deprivation and oppression.' At the same time we recognised our own weaknesses, our lack of perception and of commitment, and we hope that participation in the Process will allow us to overcome these to some extent. It is our deep conviction that it is in the churches' active response to Christ, as his body in the world, that our common future and justification lies.

On behalf of the Committee on Christian Relationships of the Religious Society of Friends in Great Britain (London Yearly Meeting)
Christine A M Davis, Clerk
Geoffrey Bowes, Recording Clerk
April 1986

Roman Catholic Church in England and Wales

Members: 1,500,000   *Ministers: 5,600*   *Churches: 3,200*

1 The Church of Christ

Sacred Scripture provides for us many images with which to reflect upon the nature of the Church. The image of the Church as the People of God, for example, finds its origins in the Old Testament (Jer 31:31-34) and its fulfilment in the New Testament (1 Peter 2:9-10). The Church is also described as the Body of Christ (1 Cor 12:12 f), the Bride of Christ (Rev. 19:7), the building of God (1 Cor 3:9), the Temple of the Holy Spirit (1 Cor: 3:16) constructed on the foundation of the apostles with Christ as its cornerstone (Eph 2:19). These and other images of the Church are mutually complementary and highlight the basic fact that the Church derives its life and meaning through in and with Christ. The Church is the Church of Christ. He is always present with his Church and lives in it as risen Lord. He calls the Church to its final fulfilment, and he gives to the Church that fundamental unity, which though marred by sinfulness and division has never been totally lost and must, in fulfilment of his will, be brought to perfection.

2 The Mission of the Church

The primary mission of the Church is to proclaim and bear witness to the good and joyful news of the love of God, poured out in creation, shown in the history of salvation and reaching its summit in the fulness of time in the life and death and resurrection of Jesus. In union with Jesus, the Church proclaims the Word through whom all things were made and through whom alone all creation will find its proper fulfilment. Jesus Christ, the Word of God made flesh reveals both the truth of God and the mystery of the human person called to an eternal destiny.

In this task the Church seeks 'to uncover, and cherish and enoble all that is true, good and beautiful in the human condition' (Second Vatican Council: Pastoral Constitution on the Church in the World Today, No 76). Such positive human developments help not only to reveal the true dignity of the human person but also to draw creation nearer to Christ who alone transforms all things into the new creation. Similarly, a fundamental task of the Church is at all times to defend basic human rights, to protest against injustice, to challenge all that is inhuman and to have a special care for the poor and oppressed.

The Church is to be the sacrament of the world's salvation. The Church is to be that place in which the holiness of creation is recognised, blessed and celebrated; in which the sinfulness of creation is acknowledged, forgiveness and healing sought. The Church is to be the sign and instrument of the coming Kingdom of God, effecting on earth that communion and reconciliation of people with God and of people with one another which are the marks of the reign of Christ. Such a mission requires that the Church must 'follow constantly the path of penance and renewal' (Second Vatican Council: Dogmatic Constitution on the Church, No 8) so that it may be seen as the sign of hope for all people.

3 The Roman Catholic Church

In a most significant manner the Second Vatican Council spoke about the relationship of the Roman Catholic Church to the Church of Christ. 'This sole Church of Christ, which the Creed we profess to be one, holy, catholic and apostolic, which our Saviour after his resurrection entrusted to Peter's pastoral care, commissioning him and the other apostles to extend and rule it.... constituted and organised as a society in this present world, subsists in the Catholic Church which is governed by the successor of Peter and by the Bishops in communion with him.' (Second Vatican Council: Dogmatic Constitution on the Church, No 8). Though carefulyy circumscribed, this statement expresses our belief that the Church of Christ is historically embodied in all its essential elements in the Roman Catholic Church, without substantial corruption or defect, however imperfectly. We accept also that the Church of Christ is not co-extensive with the Roman Catholic Church. We recognise sanctification and truth existing in other Christian communities which have a real degree of ecclesiality and are rightly called Churches.

The constituent elements of the Church of Christ we hold to be integrity of faith, acceptance of the creeds of early centuries, possession of valid sacraments and an ordained ministry within the apostolic succession. We hold that these qualities subsist in the Roman Catholic Church but not to the exclusion of some of them being present in other Churches, some at times with greater clarity. Such other Churches do possess some of the 'most significant elements and endowments which together go to build up and give life to the Church itself' (Second Vatican Council: Decree on Ecumenism, No 3). This is why we do say that the one Church of Christ indeed finds an expression in them, though in different ways.

It is expressly taught by us that, ecumenism is essential to the life of the Roman Catholic Church. We come to the work of ecumenism not with the intention of trying to achieve an amalgam of Churches but of working with others to build up into its proper fulness the one Church of Christ. We accept that within the Church of Christ there will be legitimate diversity, and different expressions of the same faith which illuminate the one truth. Formulae of faith of the past can be re-examined in a broader historical context. In such a process of dialogue, diversity can lead to our mutual enrichment. We view this task with urgency, and recall the Pope's words in Liverpool, May 1982: "Restoration of unity among Christians is one of the main aims of the Church in the last part of the twentieth century, and this task is for all. No-one can claim exemption from this responsibility." It is an urgent task because the present situation openly contradicts the will of Christ and provides a serious stumbling block in the mission given by Christ to his Church.

4 The Church as 'Koinonia'

Our understanding of the nature and mission of the Church is well expressed in the description of the Church as '*koinonia*' or '*communio*'. The primary '*koinonia*', from which the Church draws its life, is the Triune God, the prototype of unity and diversity, the perfect relationships of love, given and received. It is this reality which is lived and shared by the baptised who are thus members of the Body of Christ and in whom dwells and acts the Holy Spirit. The '*communio*' which is the Church is brought into being by the proclamation of the Word and is effected and lived in the Eucharist. Through baptism all the faithful share in the mission of Christ. Christ's people are called to be a priestly people, sanctifying all things through their active faith; they are to be a kingly people, bringing to the world the order of faith and life given in the Gospel; they are to be a prophetic people, proclaiming the Word of God with courage and in the face of opposition. All the baptised share immediately, by their own right, in this mission, and are nourished by the preaching of the Word, the celebration of the Eucharist and a life of prayer.

5 Apostolic

The preaching of the Word and celebration of the Eucharist, in our belief, require an apostolic element for their full authenticity. This quality of apostolicity we see to be one of the God given qualities of the Church of Christ subsisting in the Roman Catholic Church. Through this gift, the Church maintains, in its life and worship, fidelity to the faith, witness and mission of the apostles and seeks to transmit that fidelity to the Church of tomorrow. In our understanding this apostolicity is not simply a general quality of the faith expressed by the community but it is embodied in certain individuals, and guaranteed by the apostolic succession of the ordained ministry. To be sure of fidelity to our apostolic origins we must ask, with St Irenaeus, not only "Where is true doctrine?" but also "Where are true apostles?"

Whilst this is not to deny that the quality of apostolicity is present in some real measure in other Churches, it is to assert that we see in the bishop the authentic expression of apostolic ministry. This ministry assures us that the Word spoken and the

Eucharist celebrated are indeed of the Church of Christ. The bishop is, then, above all else the one who serves the unity of the Church. He is the 'man of communion'.

For these reasons '*Lumen Gentium*' asserts: "This Church of Christ is truly present in all legitimate local congregations which, united with their pastors, are themselves called Churches in the New Testament.... In them the faithful are gathered together by the preaching of the Gospel of Christ and the mystery of the Lord's supper is celebrated 'that by the flesh and blood of the Lord's body the whole brotherhood may be joined together'" (Second Vatican Council: Dogmatic Constitution on the Church, No 26). The Church is realised and made present in all its reality in the local Church wherever the Eucharist is authentically celebrated. In this vision there is 'a large variety of languages, of ritual forms, of historical traditions, of local prerogatives, of spiritual currents, of legitimate institutions and preferred activities' (Pope Paul IV in his inaugural address at the second session of Vatican II). Such pluriformity is a richness and strengthens the Church as the sign and sacrament of unity.

6 Catholicity

The authentic proclamation of the Word and celebration of the Eucharist bring with them an openness to the wide pluriformity of God's gifts and inclusion into the catholicity or universality of faith and communion. Those who guarantee the apostolicity of the Word and Eucharist are also an effective sign of this universality and catholicity. The bishop of the local or particular church, by virtue of his ordination, is a member of the episcopal college. This college, taken as a whole, is the successor of the group of apostles. As a member of this college, each bishop assumes a responsibility for the universal Church and is the sign that each particular church lives in communion with every other. In this wider communion of communions, we believe that the See of Rome has been given a vital and unique role: that of being the visible focus and expression of the unity of the whole Church. The primacy of the Pope is that of the head of the college of bishops. He bears prime responsibility for upholding 'communio' among the bishops, and in this way exercise his Petrine ministry within the universal Church, confirming the faith of his fellow bishops and through them, of the whole Church. We recall with gladness the manner in which the visit of Pope John Paul II to Great Britain in 1982 illustrated and confirmed this role. We also hold that the office of Pope carries with it both the defined teaching responsibility and the appropriate gifts of the Spirit necessary for its discharge. We believe, therefore, that ecclesial communion with Peter and his successor is not an obstacle to, but an anticipation and sign of, a fuller unity. We welcome the opportunity of discussing this further, recognising that our understanding of episcopacy and primacy remains a problem for some of the Churches with which we are in dialogue, and conscious that some of these difficulties arise from our failures in the past.

7 Tradition and Authority

These qualities of apostolicity and catholicity in 'koinonia' are the foundation for order and authority in the Church. Throughout history, living and believing men and women, who make up the Church, deepen, develop and hand on their faith in succeeding generations, and express it in manifold ways. The Spirit is present in the Church, unfolding the truth of the Gospel message and bringing forth its fruit.

Despite shameful and damaging periods in our history, a fundamental conviction of the Roman Catholic Church is that it has never been allowed by Christ to adopt formally a position which is incompatible with the Truth it is called to serve. No matter how defective its theory or practice at any particular time, when the Church has committed itself to judgements in fundamental matters of faith, we believe that the Spirit of Christ has protected it from error. "A universal council and the universal primate, presiding over the 'koinonia' and speaking with authority, are both agencies through which the Church can so act" (Bishops' Conference of England and Wales: Response to ARCIC, para 34). We believe that the exercise of the discernment of faith by the bishops, especially when acting together in union with the Pope, or in certain circumstances by the Pope himself, is an essential element in the formulation of doctrinal statements. We find it difficult to see a similar fulfilment of this function in some other Churches. This is not to cast doubts upon the beliefs of those other Churches but to question the manner in which those beliefs are formulated and established. We do believe that the nature of the authority exercised in the Roman Catholic Church by Pope and bishops, is part of God's design for the Church. This is not to defend the manner in which that authority has always been exercised, nor to deny that other types of authority can and do emerge, for example, the personal authority of outstanding individuals. It is to assert that our understanding of the Church as '*communio*' leads us to believe that this type of episcopal authority is one of the constituent elements of the Church of Christ. We recognise that this whole question needs to be handled with great sensitivity. We are a pilgrim Church living in a time of cultural pluralism and change. We acknowledge our need to learn and grow in knowledge and self-realisation.

8 Sacraments and the Church

The Church of Christ is the sacrament of salvation for the world. The communion of life between God and the baptised which is the heart of the life of the Church is the sign and sacrament of the unity, reconciliation and peace which is intended by God for all people. Thus the life of the Church, in all its concrete reality, is to be an effective sign of that 'communion of life' to which all people aspire. As the Second Vatican Council in its Dogmatic Constitution on the Church states:

'The society furnished with hierarchical agencies and the mystical body of Christ are not to be considered as two realities; rather they form one, interlocking reality, which comes together from a human and divine element' (8). The Church of Christ, subsisting in the Roman Catholic Church, has been established by him as a visible structure, bringing together the divine and human elements. The Church then belongs to that historical realisation, in a visible historical form, of God's secret plan to gather all people and the entire universe into the unity of his Kingdom. The structured life of the Church is, then, rooted in the nature of the Church as sacrament, rooted in the incarnate life of God and is part of the way in which the Church is to be the sacrament of salvation for the world.

The life of the believer and of the community of faith are marked then by moments in which this sacramental nature of the Church is expressed in a specific and precise manner. Thus the greatest events in our spiritual life take place through the sacraments when we celebrate the life of God penetrating to the roots of human existence. The sacrament of baptism is the most significant moment in our lives when the life-giving water of the Holy Spirit transforms us into sons and daughters of God and makes us members of the body of Christ. All that happens subsequently is a matter of growing more fully into this saving communion of life. In confirmation, we are called upon to renew that profession of our faith made at our baptism, but, of all sacraments, we look upon the Eucharist as the climax because here we assemble as the Body of Christ, the risen head, and worship through, with and in him. In the Eucharist the Sacrifice of Christ, recalled and proclaimed, is made effective here and now. In the Eucharist Christ offers himself as our true food and drink. United with Christ in the Eucharist, we are united with each other in the depth of our being. In the sacrament of reconciliation, we come to know in a personal way the forgiving heart of Christ which touches the deepest areas of alienation in our lives. By anointing with oil and laying on of hands, we meet the healing power of Jesus Christ in those of us weighed down by sickness of mind and body. Finally, the sacraments of priesthood and matrimony celebrate and mark out the ways in which some are called to serve God in the life of the community.

These sacraments, celebrated in the Roman Catholic Church with the guarantee of its apostolicity and catholicity, nourish, sustain and build up the community of faith so that the witness of its life will more readily proclaim in society the presence of God's saving love.

We rejoice in being able to recognise that in the sacrament of baptism, celebrated in the name of Father, Son and Holy Spirit, a bond of real communion is established between believers. This is the basis of the real but incomplete communion existing now between Churches: a communion nourished by our sharing of the Word of God, prayer and service of the world. We look forward to the day when this communion will be such as to find true expression in full Eucharistic communion between us.

9 The Call to Holiness

The mission given by Christ to his Church involves an invitation to every person to a life of union with God in and through Christ by the power of the Spirit. Such holiness of life is the primary form of witness to be given by the Church and corresponds to our belief that the only way the world can be healed is through the effective and saving presence of Christ. In this work of salvation Catholics believe that they depend utterly on the grace of God yet they must co-operate with that grace through a life of generous effort, mutual help, self-control and at times self-denial.

In this light the Roman Catholic Church has always professed itself to be a Church of sinners. "In all that it does, in its life of prayer and witness, in its discipline and its demands, the Church must have regard for the frailty which people so often experience. The Church must reflect at all times the mind of Jesus Christ when he said 'It is not the healthy who need the doctor but the sick. Go and learn the meaning of the words: What I want is mercy, not sacrifice. And indeed I did not come to call the virtuous but sinners' (Matthew 9:12.23)" (Bishops' Conference of England and Wales: The Easter People, para 22). This awareness gives rise in the Church to an urgency in seeking the forgiveness of God and the conversion of heart and mind that the Gospel constantly demands.

Mary, the Mother of Jesus, is pre-eminent in the life of the Church called to holiness. In her, above all, we are able to recognise the model of discipleship for all. The privilege of her

Immaculate Conception is a real symbol of freedom from the domination of sin. Her bodily Assumption to heaven is a symbol of that bodily resurrection which Christ, as the first-fruits from the dead, will one day offer to all creation. We rejoice in her company and in that of the saints of every age. As a Preface of the Roman Missal says: 'You, Lord, are glorified in your saints, for their glory is the crowning of your gifts. In their lives on earth you give us an example. In our communion with them you give us their friendship. In their prayer for the Church you give us their strength and protection.' This great company of witnesses spurs us on our pilgrim way, and encourages us in our desire to fulfil the prayer of Christ that we may all be one.

Russian Orthodox Church

Members: 1,500   *Ministers: 5*   *Churches: 5*

How do you understand the nature and purpose of your Church in relation to other Christian denominations?

The Russian Orthodox believe: that there is only one Church, which is the 'body of Christ'. Together all the autocephalous Orthodox churches are the visible Church, Catholic and Apostolic, and instituted by our Lord Jesus Christ Himself and the holy apostles. Orthodox churches do not generally make a distinction between the Church visible and the Church invisible believing this to be a tacit denial of the Incarnation. With humility, and yet with conviction, the Orthodox Church believes that the Church of Christ was an historically constituted event by the Holy Spirit on the Day of Pentecost. The Orthodox Church believes that it is still that constituted Church.

However, it is also the case to quote tradition 'that we know where the Holy Spirit is, but we do not say where He is not.' The Orthodox Church does not own God the Holy Spirit, and He 'bloweth where He listeth.' Consequently in our dealings with other churches we look for the marks of the Spirit: of love, of repentance, and seek to relate these to the 'right believing' of the apostolic faith as set forth in the Nicene Creed. Whilst we seek good relations with Christians everywhere, we feel particularly drawn to all those denominations that seek to preserve and promote the gospel of our Lord Jesus Christ untainted by modernist interpretations.

…and as we share in God's mission to the world?

Sharing in God's mission presupposes a common understanding of mission and Church. What is the Church and its mission is probably the central ecumenical question of our time. The

Russian Orthodox church represents what might be called a 'primitive' approach to Christianity. We believe that our emphasis on liturgy and prayer and above all our experience of the eschatalogical dimension of faith is a witness to mission perhaps most needed in the west. Conversely, Orthodoxy – through the *diaspora* – is only just beginning to wear a western face: it needs to listen and learn what others know of Christ. Perhaps all Christian denominations in order to become involved in God's mission to the world need to talk and listen in order to find out what sharing together means.

Salvation Army

Members: 65,000 *Ministers: 3,900* *Churches: 930*

SUMMARY STATEMENT

1. The church universal comprises all true believers in Jesus Christ.

2. Believers stand in a spiritual relationship to one another which is not dependent upon any particular church structure.

3. The Salvation Army is part of the church universal and a Christian denomination called into and sustained in being by God.

4. Denominational variety is not self-evidently contrary to God's will for His people.

5. Inter-denominational harmony and co-operation are valuable for the enriching of the life and witness of each denomination.

6. The Salvation Army welcomes inter-church involvement in every land where the Army is established.

AMPLIFIED STATEMENT

The Church Universal

1. *WE BELIEVE* that the church, the body of Christ (Ephesians 1:23), comprises all who are born not of blood, nor of the will of the flesh, nor of the will of man, but of God (John 1:13). The church universal includes all who believe in the Lord Jesus Christ and confess Him as Lord.

   WE DO NOT BELIEVE that the church universal depends for its existence or validity upon any particular ecclesiastical structure, any particular form of worship, or any particular observance of ritual.

2. *WE BELIEVE* that the church universal is the whole of the worshipping, witnessing Christian community throughout the centuries into whatever groupings, large or small, accepted or persecuted, wealthy or poor, her members may have been structured in the past or are governed in the present.

    WE DO NOT BELIEVE that an adequate definition of the church can be confined in terms of ecclesiastical structure, but must rather be stated in terms of a spiritual relationship. Members of the church are those who are incorporate in Christ Jesus (Ephesians 1:1) and therefore reconciled to God through His Son. All such are in a spiritual relationship one with the other which begins and continues regardless of externals, according to the prayer of Jesus that those who are His may be one (John 17:23). These words of Jesus ask for a oneness as is found in the oneness of Father and Son. This oneness is spiritual, not organizational.

3. *WE BELIEVE* that The Salvation Army is part of the church universal and a representative of the body of Christ. Christ is the True Vine (John 15:1) and believers are His living, fruit-bearing branches.

    WE DO NOT BELIEVE that any community of true followers of Christ can rightly be regarded as outside the church universal, whatever their history, customs or practices when set in comparison with those of other Christian communities. God alone knows those who are truly His (2 Timothy 2:19).

Denominational Variety

4. *WE BELIEVE* that God's dealings with His people are perfect according to His will, but that human responses are imperfect and prone to error. It may be God's dealings or fallible human responses to those dealings which have

brought about the rich and varied denominational tapestry discernible today.

WE DO NOT BELIEVE that denominational or organizational variety can automatically and in every case be said to be contrary to God's will for His people.

5. *WE BELIEVE* that God raised up The Salvation Army according to His purposes for His glory and the proclamation of the gospel.

WE DO NOT BELIEVE that The Salvation Army's existence as an independent and distinctive Christian community, having no formal, structural ties with other Christian communities, is an affront to the gospel of Jesus Christ or self-evidently contrary to God's will for the whole of His body on earth.

6. *WE BELIEVE* that the practices of The Salvation Army have much in common with the practices of other churches, but that being raised up by God for a distinctive work, the Army has been led to adopt the following combination of characteristics:

   a) its emphasis upon personal religion and individual spiritual regeneration through faith in Christ leading in turn to a commitment to seek to win others to Christ;

   b) its teaching concerning holy living;

   c) its insistence that the gospel is for the whosoever;

   d) its use of the Mercy Seat;

   e) its avoidance of set-forms in worship, seeking to encourage spontaneity;

   f) its teaching that the receiving of inward spiritual grace is not dependent upon any particular outward observance;

   g) its requirement that full members (soldiers) publicly confess their faith in Jesus Christ as their Saviour and Lord, and enter into a formal doctrinal and ethical commitment, the latter including abstention from alcohol, tobacco, and non-medical use of addictive drugs;

h) its encouragement into Army fellowship of those unable to enter into the formal commitment of soldiership;

i) its strong commitment to evangelism, including outdoor evangelism;

j) its witness through the wearing of distinctive uniform on the part of most salvationists;

k) its recognition of the equal place of women and men in all aspects of Christian ministry and leadership;

l) its tradition of service to the needy;

m) its world-wide structure and its emphasis upon internationalism;

n) its use of brass music in worship and evangelism.

These are part of the blessings which have come through God's gracious dealings with us through the years.

WE DO NOT BELIEVE it to be self-evidently God's will for His people in the Army that they cast aside in haste the blessings of the years.

The Local Church

7. *WE BELIEVE* that just as the true church universal comprises all who believe on the Lord Jesus Christ, so each denominational church comprises a community of true believers who have in common the way the Lord, who through His Holy Spirit has dealt with them as a community. In turn, each denominational church comprises local churches regularly meeting together for worship, fellowship and service in a relatively confined geographical location.

WE DO NOT BELIEVE that the validity of a denomination or its local churches depends upon any particular ecclesiastical tradition, structure, hierarchy, form of worship, or ritual. Where even two or three gather in Christ's name there He is present (Matthew 18:20) with a presence no less real than that discerned in larger, more formal or ritualistic settings.

The Army's Identity

8. *WE BELIEVE* that The Salvation Army is an international Christian denomination with other Christian denominations and that the Army's local corps are local churches with the local churches of other Christian denominations. The Army springs from the Methodist revival and has remained unassimilated by any other denomination.

   WE DO NOT BELIEVE that The Salvation Army's history, structures, practices or beliefs permit it to be understood as anything other than a distinct Christian denomination with a purpose to fulfil and a calling to discharge under God. Similarly, its local corps cannot properly be understood unless seen primarily as local churches meeting regularly in Christ's name for worship, fellowship and service. Commissioned officers (both men and women) of The Salvation Army are ministers of the Christian gospel, called by God and empowered by the Holy Spirit to preach and teach apostolic truth in the name of Christ and for His sake.

The Army and Other Churches

9. *WE BELIEVE* that it is God's will that harmonious relations are built up and sustained, by His grace, between Christians everywhere and between all Christian denominations including their local churches. The Army's numerous and widespread contacts with other Christian communities both in Britain and around the world serve to enrich the Army's spirituality and to enhance its understanding of the work of the Spirit. For this reason the Army welcomes such contacts and seeks cordially to extend and deepen them.

   WE DO NOT BELIEVE that narrowness or exclusiveness are consistent with God's will for His people, or that God has nothing to teach us by our sharing and co-operating with His people in other denominations.

10. *WE BELIEVE* that every visible unit of the Church universal is endowed with its own blessings and strengths as gifts from God. We respect, and in many cases admire, those strengths recognizing too that because of human frailty every denomination, including The Salvation Army, has its imperfections.

    WE DO NOT BELIEVE it is our task or place to criticize or undermine the traditions or emphases of other denominations, and certainly not in relation to the sacraments on which our stance is unusual, though not unique. It is contrary to our practices to offer hostile comment upon the life of any denomination or local church.

    We are anxious not to belittle the doctrines or practices of any other Christian group. The Army places emphasis in its teaching not upon externals but upon the need for each believer personally to experience that inward spiritual grace to which the external observance testifies. We maintain that no external observance can rightly be said to be essential to salvation and that the biblical truth is that we can meet with God and receive His grace anywhere at any time.

11 *WE BELIEVE* The Salvation Army was called into being by the will of God, is sustained in being by God's grace, and is empowered for obedience by the Holy Spirit. Its overriding purpose is to win the souls of men and women and boys and girls for God, whilst working simultaneously, and for Christ's sake, to alleviate the material lot of those in need.

    WE DO NOT BELIEVE that we alone are called to this sacred and awesome task and therefore we rejoice that in other Christian churches we find co-workers for God.

Shiloh United Church of Christ

Members: 18,000 *Ministers: 46* *Churches: 10*★*

★ Not owned, but leased or rented (e.g. halls belonging to other Churches)
(figures supplied by the Shiloh United Church of Christ)

Question

(A) In your tradition and experience, how do you understand the nature and purpose of your church (or churches when the national body is a federation of local churches)?
(B) In relation to other Christian denominations
(C) And as we share in God's Mission to the world

The three part question above is not an easy one to answer in respect of free thinking allowed in our churches. The Shiloh United Church of Christ Apostolic Worldwide is a federal body – every church is sovereign in itself, and although there is one earthly head and an agreed Biblical Scripture's Foundation on which we are based and unite. Each Pastor or Overseer is free to serve his church as being led of the Holy Spirit, we have no set liturgy nationally.

I personally could answer the question without difficulty but for our churches it is not easy. The whole setting is very complex because our whole attitude to the Ministry is so different. To us Mission is an on-going labour of love from January to December, on and on because we see Mission as our Number One job in this world.

Concerning the Christian denominations, there should be no line drawn but unfortunately, interpretation and certain practices in certain denominations is unacceptable to us, and although we respect them for what they are and are able to join hands in serving our communities in the secular field, a vital link is broken.

My sum-total is that we continue to respect each other, exercising our God qualities and putting in the full effect – Eph. 4:3.

The Lord bless you.

Unitarian and Free Christian Churches

Members: 9,000   *Ministers: 170*   *Churches: 240*

The Unitarian Response

Background

1. The first object of the General Assembly of Unitarian and Free Christian Churches, formed in 1928 from other bodies, is "to promote pure Religion in the Worship of God and the Service of Man." An association of churches, formed chiefly in the 17th – 19th centuries, the Assembly has no executive or coercive powers in terms of practice or belief over churches or individuals. It speaks for organised Unitarianism in the British Isles but its functions are purely representational and advisory. The individual church gathering can and does speak and comment on behalf of itself but in doing this does not bind or limit the thought, feelings or expression of the members or anyone else. Authority in our understanding and practice lies with the individual taking personal responsibility. All statements made by people within or through organisations on behalf of others who consider themselves Unitarian are therefore qualified and lacking in finality, both in theory and practice.

The nature and purpose of the church

2. The nature and purpose of the local gathered church is not clearly defined, nor ever has been. It can however be summarised in the following broad aims:

To bring like-minded people together for worship and mutual support, developing spiritual awareness and bonds of community as they share their religious journey through life. This means that Unitarians essentially build their own theology, and while looking to the local church and its minister to guide them in this lifelong effort, the final responsibility for their spiritual, moral and social future is their own. They may be guided by a spiritual reality but see this as contained within themselves. All Unitarians stand on their own feet in religious terms though it is recognised that some are more able to do this than others. The local church, through its worship and ministry, encompasses this variety of need by means of inspiration, prompting an encouragement though it never demands or requiries.

To affirm the worth and dignity of every person, which entails the spread and advance of justice, equality and democratic process. For the local church this means that all are equal, that nobody is set apart with special privileges, nor is any person in membership of that church lesser or greater in any way than another. A minister may be set apart in function, but not in any other way.

To present and nurture the eternal truths as well as the latest scientific thinking, and in a critical but supportive atmosphere to venture, in as open a manner as possible without an unhealthy fear or sense of guilt, into the unknown future. Organised Unitarianism promotes and defends the free and disciplined search for truth and meaning wherever it may lead, believing that this is an imperative for the wholeness and vitality of the human spirit. It follows from this that churches do not limit the range or extent of enquiry. Thus creeds are rarely to be found, and all orthodoxies of thinking whether personal or collective are open to challenge.

To foster spiritual growth and the loving acceptance of our fellow human beings, in the understanding that this is central to our ideal of religious community, and to express this vision to those beyond our community in whatever ways we can in the spirit of service. This means that the local church lives in the world, not separated off in its own structures and we hope and believe it to be a useful part of society. Few Unitarians see themselves or their churches as having a mission to proclaim the worth of their beliefs to others, though they do wish to present their faith to others as a vital and living one. Because we see ourselves as part of a religiously pluralistic society, we do not feel the need to try to change it on preconceived religious lines. Personal service rather than collective action is our ideal.

3. While these may be considered as the aims of the local church, it cannot be said that we always live up to our aspirations. However these benchmarks can be used to help in the process of examining the nature and purpose of our churches today. Any conclusions reached on our relationship to the Christian denominations and in "mission" to the world must be based on these aims.

4. The nature of our relationship to the various Christian denominations depends essentially on the view that the local church or individual Unitarian takes of their own connection with and to the tenets of Christianity. This view or attitude in the British Isles is enormously varied but can be considered to lie in three main areas:

a. Those who emphasise the insights of the Judaic and Christian traditions, but who reject virtually all the traditional creeds and formularies or orthodox Christianity as binding or authoritative. They embrace what might be termed as a modern liberal Christian theological standpoint. These Unitarians, and the local churches in which they form a majority, see Christianity as "the quarry whence we were digged" and generally use Christian imagery to express their religious ideals. In spirit they see themselves as part of the universal Christian church.

b. Those who affirm a belief in a spiritual force expressed in the wisdom and prophecy of both East and West, but not necessarily in Christian terms. Some of these Unitarians are theists or deists, while many others believe in aspects of one or other of the great world faiths (or a combination of them) that accord with their personal spiritual awareness.

c. Those who affirm the humanistic tradition of the Western world, believing that the traditional gods are no longer adequate models of spiritual value and place particular emphasis on human reason, a fuller self-understanding of our motives and needs and a greater sense of social responsibility to improve the human condition.

5. While these are not exclusive or watertight compartments, and it would be difficult to categorise many Unitarians in this way, these classifications represent the broad groupings of Unitarian religious thinking today and hence its attitude towards the Christian denominations. Because the number of Unitarians in each category is significant, it is not possible to express a single Unitarian view of the Christian denominations. While authoritative Unitarian statements are impossible, viewpoints on this question are particularly varied. All that can be given is a likely view of the reaction of each category to the question of how they understand the nature and purpose of the Unitarian church in relation to the Christian denominations.

6. The question itself raises a problem, as the last two categories do not see Unitarianism as an exclusively Christian denomination. Consequently they believe the word "other" in the question to be inappropriate. The old question asked since the 18th century, "Are Unitarians Christians?" is generally today sidestepped even by those who affirm the Christian nature of our tradition. Many Unitarians believe it to be a meaningless question as it depends on the view of Christianity taken by the questioner rather than the answer given. Others wish to maintain the Christian association but cannot see that the exclusion of Unitarians from the 'Christian fold' by those who proclaim a very different theology as to be of any meaning.

Unitarians and their churches with the liberal Christian viewpoint often find considerable meaning and value in their relations with other Christian denominations. They are often members of local Councils of Churches, taking an active part where this is possible. Their viewpoint of the nature and purpose of the church may not be very different from that of some other denominations, except in theological terms which is often the key difference. Thus while our churches in this category are very willing to co-operate, collectively or individually, they would not be willing to link up or come together under what might be termed an orthodox Christian banner. They are often at one with Christian denominations in the Christian spirit, but hardly ever in the letter of the Christian 'law'.

8. Those Unitarians whose viewpoint is theistic or religiously pluralistic take a more detached view of the denominations. While few take a hostile stance, most see the Christian denominations as part of the old religious order which many have left to become Unitarian. This grouping tends to stress the religious spirit behind the observances of any religious tradition; if this spirit is 'right' then they feel at one with those of similar spirit. This, they believe, can be found amongst Buddhists and Hindus, for example, as it can amongst the Christians, and they tend to look at all the denominations in this light. The theists "cannot shut God up in any denomination". They do not essentially believe that we are a Christian denomination, though most are willing to associate with Christian churches through bodies like the British Council of Churches.

9. Unitarians who are humanistic in thought and feeling may not see themselves in any way as part of the church universal. Although many may have memories of an orthodox, hymn singing past, they often have a moderately hostile view of Christianity. Seeing Unitarianism and its churches as having a distinct social and moral standpoint, they view participation in events with Christian churches in anything but social responsibility matters as a sham. They would like Unitarians to leave such bodies as the BCC, local Councils of Churches etc. They believe that the spirit of our movement is such that we should disassociate ourselves from the Christian "umbrella".

10. Most Unitarians see the nature and purpose of their church as being similar in spirit to that of the Christian denominations, and are very willing to co-operate in appropriate joint ventures. Many feel a special affinity with the Society of Friends for a variety of reasons, most of which do not seem to be theological. There are numerous examples of joint membership.

11. In concluding this section it needs to be pointed out that the proposals for church unity put forward over the last twenty years have had little or no impact on Unitarians or their churches. Any future efforts in this direction, however conducted, are likely to have a similar impact. We see the nature

and purpose of our churches as distinct, and our witness to be a separate one now and in the future, whatever the Christian denominations might do to join together. We know, for example, of no Unitarian who would accept the creedal statement contained in the Constitution of the BCC, except in the broadest symbolic terms.

Sharing God's mission to the world

12. Unitarians are uneasy with the word 'mission', possibly unreasonably so, taking it to be a term associated with the spreading of what they see as a narrow form of Christianity by certain dubious methods developed in the 19th century. Mission in terms of 'proclaiming what is believed to be true' cannot be objected to but it is a word that Unitarians shy away from, and generally avoid its use. Those engaging in dialogue with us will need to take this factor into consideration; the word 'evangelism' raises similar problems.

13. As may be gathered, a large number of Unitarians do not believe in an external god who could have a mission to the world, a view seemingly shared by certain modern Christian theologians. Thus most Unitarians would have considerable difficulty with the phraseology of this part of the question, though many would have sympathy with the meaning behind it.

14. The use and understanding of Christian terminology has long provided problems for Unitarians. Taking this fact into consideration, it can be said that most Unitarians believe that all denominations are on a similar quest, and are at one where that quest involves those who are honestly and sincerely seeking to create a better world and a truer and more real spiritual understanding. Most Unitarians however find that there are groups who share our vision of this quest who are not churches or even specifically religious. The multi-faith Britain of today means there are larger numbers of such groups with whom we feel we can make common cause. We thus look wider than the Christian horizon; the Christian world is included in our spiritual view though it is seen as but part of the picture. Indeed we are all pilgrims on the way but each with a different vision

needs to take a different path. There is "unity, not in a common creed, but a common quest." (Radhakrishnan). We can be strangers even to those who share our pathway. The need is to recognise that those on a different pathway have a spiritual integrity which must be recognised by all, even though the paths may seemingly be going in opposite directions.

Alan Ruston

United Reformed Church

Members: 135,000   *Ministers: 1,620*   *Churches: 1,860*

A Statement from the United Reformed Church on the nature and purpose of the Church in the light of its mission

1. Dust and Spirit

Like all churches we are a mixed bag and we have our differences. To present a comprehensive portrait in a small space is impractical; it would need a travelling camera to produce a long school photo. But for some people in the URC the church means a gathering for worship on Sunday morning, in a sanctuary built in the 1890's with about 60 people present and with a minister preaching a sermon thoughtfully offered and leading prayers deeply felt. That expression of the church is a reality but does not tell the whole story. In this account of the URC we recognise the weakness of our discipleship, fellowship and witness, but also look at the calling of God as we have received it, the many gifts shared among us and our expectation as we explore God's mission in the world.

That note of the mixture which we sense in all church life points us to the mystery of the church. At every point it is both flesh and spirit, dust of the earth and breath of God. We see the human institution with its rules and buildings, but also the glorious company of the apostles, martyrs and saints in whom God's spirit has been made plain in the world. Our response to God in faith, partial though it is, is our entry into the pilgrimage of his people, with all the discipline and joy that entails, but the end of which is not visible to us nor ours to command.

It is this experience which shapes our understanding of church and Kingdom. The church is a consequence of the Gospel, the community where the story of Jesus is celebrated, the presence of Jesus is known, the healing of Jesus is brought into human lives and the way of the cross is proclaimed and practised throughout the world. God's purpose, as we know it, is that his church might so bear his truth and his nature that it demonstrates the new life in Christ for all the world to see. It is a first instalment of the Kingdom, where love controls relationships and hope directs vision. The failures of the church, in all ages and in all its branches, remind is that, like Paul, we have not yet reached the mark but press on towards it, and need forgiveness at every step. Exclusive claims for the church sit uneasily beside the breadth of God's love and the uncontrollable wind of Spirit, but great claims for Christ are the ground of our praise.

2. By what authority?

To speak of the URC as a church and part of the church is a considerable claim which implies some authority to make it. God's authority is both over the church, to judge and cleanse it, and through the church, to proclaim his word in the world. Any authority in the people of God derives from his presence with them. We believe that his presence is known as we study the bible and celebrate the sacraments, as we receive the experience of Christians through the ages and as we respond to his call in our own lives. These are not mechanical channels, they are personal and therefore limited by our dim vision, like 'puzzling reflections in a mirror'. (1 Cor: 13.12) We do not claim God's authority to judge or exclude or declare the whole of truth. But the presence of God has been so real for our community of faith that we believe we have authority to declare the Gospel, to celebrate the sacraments, to shape church life and to make decisions, both corporate and individual, about the way of the Kingdom in the affairs of the world. We do not hold any written creed to be a test of faith, but a witness to faith as it was understood at one moment in history. We have to make our own testimony, in life as well as in words, as pilgrims under the authority of God.

3. Apostolic, Catholic and Reformed

We believe that there is an apostolic succesion. It is the succession of faithful people which links us with the physical of Christ in Palestine, and which testifies in all ages to the power of the Holy Spirit. The church is apostolic as it lives within the confidence that Christ is risen and as it shares that faith with the world. Faithfilness to that inheritance is one of the gifts of the Spirit, and is not guaranteed – however it may be helped – by any human institution. The guarantee is the faithfulness of God.

To be catholic is the gift of God which is one of the characteristics of the church. It is the quality of wholeness – the whole Gospel presented by a whole witness for the whole world. We do not see any present communion possessing catholicity. None can claim that all the breadth of devotion and wisdom is within its borders. The divided church is not a whole church, for there is even exclusion at the Lord's table. We pray that we may be catholic as we pray for holiness, and we treasure the keynotes of catholic tradition in scripture, sacraments, ministry and faith in the risen Christ.

To be reformed is to be a part of a particular history. The Reformation was a period of dynamic movement, often confused and no doubt spoiled by intolerance and the mixed motives which lame us all. Yet it was a spiritual liberation. Breaking out from the structures of the late medieval church, men and women discovered new life in Christian communities which opened the word of God for themselves, shared freely in the sacraments and praised God in their own language. The power of that movement lay in the obedience of those who heard the word of God through scriptures as it came alive in their context, and we acknowledge that same witness in the Reformed churches of today. The very same dynamism was at work in the early nineteenth century movement which led to the Disciples (Churches of Christ).

4. The Vocation of the Church

The mission of the church in the world is easy to write about and never easy to fulfil. It means following the way of Christ, the way of self-offering. We repeatedly fall away into self-concern. Maintenance frequently threatens mission. But members of the URC would probably recognise in the following notes the main tasks to which we are called.

4.1 Praising God. We are called to worship God with love, intelligence and sincerity, so that there may be a response of deep thankfulness for God's gift of life and salvation. The focus of our worship is the Word made flesh, God's coming in the limitation and vulnerability of our humanity, so that we may be united with him in faith. We confess that worship is too often dull. We pray for the spirit of joy and hope in all our worship.

4.2 Praying with love. We are to pray, in public and in private, for those in trouble, pain and loss; to pray for the whole fellowship of Christians; to pray for our own growth in faith. In prayer the church seeks to lift up human need before God, to enter into his loving purposes and to become part of his saving hand in the world.

4.3 Sharing Good News. We are to speak the word of forgiveness to all who turn to God in sincerity. Our life as a church or as individual Christians never fully reveals the wonder of the Gospel of grace. Therefore the speaking, writing, preaching and singing of the Gospel is a constant calling, so that others may know that God reaches out to us all in Jesus.

4.4 Challenging evil. Both in the small scale of the home which is threatened by bitterness or poverty, and in the large scale of nations overcome by an ideology of death or slavery, we know something of the light which is God's presence and the darkness which is God excluded. The church is called to struggle against evil.

4.5 Serving the community. The church is called to touch the life of the world around us in the spirit of healing, reconciliation and confidence of God. This means involvement, participation, study and co-operation in the common life. In this sense the whole church is the missionary of the Gospel. We are grateful that during the last century our particular traditions have given a large place to civic duty and service. In our day this is translated into multiform involvement as local churches give room to a host of community organisations, and church members are in the frontline of social service.

How are we to hold these dimensions of our vocation together? We know how easily they can be separated. Jesus Christ came to save people, to heal and recreate and renew people, to bring the whole world into that unity with God which true life. It is in following him that we find every talent used, every piece of service becoming a prayer and every act of worship translated into love for neighbour. We know that we often fail to serve the whole Gospel, and our most common temptation is to be satisfied with our passive attendance at public worship as sufficient response to what God has done.

5. The URC – Our short life

To give a testimony for our church must include reference to this brief history. Congregational and Presbyterian churches came together in 1972 and were joined by the Re-formed Association of Churches of Christ in 1981. These acts of union were not without pain. We said farewell to some old friends who could not join us in the enterprise. There are those among us who still feel that they have lost something precious in a particular tradition. But for many this has been a time of joy, learning and enlargement, with horizons being widened. It is a young church and it often *feels* a young church. It is, perhaps, the reality of change and the constant exploration of new ways of being the church which have contributed most to the feeling that the URC is young and alive. There is a tension created, on the one hand, by the need to settle down and realise our own potential and establish our identity, and, on the other hand, the call to press forward into new exploration of how the whole church may be healed of its divisions. It is a healthy tension to live with, for it reflects the 'now' and 'not yet' of the Kingdom. The URC is not a piece of ecclesiastical territory we have won and intend to hold, but rather a bridgehead where we dare not remain and from which we are called to move forward.

6. Our emphasis

The URC sees itself as part of the whole church in these islands which is called to give expression to certain major emphases –

6.1 Reform. As a church standing in the tradition of the Reformation we have a special obligation to sustain the fundamental principle that God's Word, alive and active, constantly teaches us new ways of obedience in every human context. New light and truth do 'spring forth from God's holy word', as one English Reformer declared.

6.2 Participation. The three traditions which have come together in URC all cherished the reality of membership which carries with it the obligation to participate in the ordering of the church and in its mission in the world.

6.3 Liberty. As a small denomination which has historic experience of civil disabilities, we cherish freedom of religion. In consequence we also acknowledge the freedom of minority opinion within the URC, and the liberty of each congregation to develop its patterns of worship and mission. The limits of freedom for us as a church are set by fellowship in one body.

6.4 Unity. We feel called to encourage the process towards unity, challenging those obstacles which inhibit full fellowship and attempting new ways of expressing the reconciling grace of Christ. We have not yet seen the shape of unity which can hold all the diversity of the disciples of Christ. About 12% of our congregations are now in local unions or covenants with other denominations.

7. Membership

It is by God's grace that we become part of his church. That grace cannot be confined to our channels, so there is no human way of enumerating God's faithful people. But we do seek to know membership in the URC. The process of entering into the full responsibilities of membership includes baptism and confession of faith. Because of our union we have been led to see two forms of baptism as equivalent alternatives and both forms as proper witnesses to the Gospel. Parents may bring a child for baptism; teaching and nurture follow and we hope that a personal declaration of faith in Christ is made when the person is mature enough to make a public commitment. Alternatively parents may bring a child for a service of thanksgiving and blessing, and baptism is celebrated later on when the individual gives personal expression to faith. It is too soon to say how the breadth of practice will develop in every locality.

8. Church Order

8.1 We do not find in Scripture, in Christian history or in present experience that any one existing order is mandatory for all Christians. One aspect of our present pilgrimage is to seek that ordering of the church which will draw us closer to Christ and help us all to serve him more effectively.

8.2 In the local church there is a regular meeting of the members which is the body responsible for key decisions regarding the witness and service of the fellowship. There is also an Elders' Meeting. Elders are elected and ordained. They form a corporate leadership on the local church, and share in the pastoral care of the members. Elders normally represent the local church in the wider councils of URC.

8.3 We ordain ministers of the Word and Sacraments. They are called by one or more congregations and the District Council is responsible for concurring in the call and for inducting them to the pastorate. We have 760 stipendiary ministers, supported financially by the whole URC, and 145 auxiliary (non-stipendiary) ministers. Some ministers serve the church in central appointments and some serve overseas.

8.4 Congregations are grouped in Districts and Districts in Provinces. Each of the 12 Provincial Synods is served by a minister appointed by the General Assembly to be Moderator. The Moderator has pastoral responsibility for ministers and their families, normally presides at meetings of the Synod, and at ordinations and inductions of ministers in the Province, and is charged to 'stimulate and encourage' the work of the URC in that area. The Moderator's appointment is for a stated term.

8.5 The District Council appoint representatives to the General Assembly which meets annually and is the decision-making body for the denomination which covers England, Scotland and Wales. It is served by a central staff. It elects annually a Moderator as the national representative and president of the church, and a General Secretary is appointed for a stated term. The Assembly has a membership of about 700, half lay, half ministers.

8.6 Our experience is that God calls both women and men to every ministry of the church. Through our Congregational roots this experience extends for 70 years.

8.7 We find that individual and corporate oversight need to be blended at all levels of church life. This has long been customary in local churches. In Districts, Provinces and the national church the experience is less traditional and the URC is still working our the appropriate balance.

9. Relationships with other Christians

9.1 Part and Whole. Since there is only one church of Jesus Christ, we know that our own communion is only a small fragment of the whole. We recognise Christian faith and devotion in a host of others. As the fragment receives God's mercy in the Gospel it does not preach a fragment of salvation, but points to the wholeness of life in Christ. When a local church joins in prayer at a baptism, for example, the members represent the whole people of God, in the apostolic tradition, and seek the fulness of Christ's blessing for the person being baptised. But our knowledge of Christ is incomplete. Only 'with all the saints' shall we understand and receive the full dimensions of the love of Christ.

9.2 Fellowship now. There is much we share as expressions of unity – baptism in the name of the Trinity, the celebration of the Lord's Supper to which we commonly welcome members of all the churches, ministers of the Word and Sacraments, the open Bible, prayers and praises, the great Christian festivals and common service for those in need. When an ordained minister of another church seeks entry into the URC ministry we do not ordain again, for we understand the church which has ordained to have acted for the whole church. Similarly we are able to receive a member without a further act of confirmation.

9.3 Ecumenical movement. We give thanks for this movement which has enabled us to enter more fully into the breadth of God's family. It can be a painful process as we learn how we have hurt others, and as we witness the struggles of other Christians whom we have done little to assist. 'With all the saints' does not mean a party for mutual congratulations. We learn most from those experiences when we hear different views of Christ and when others speak the truth in love to us. Ecumenism is also a joy as we discover closeness in the Lord.

9.4 World Mission. Many of our world links have grown out of the missionary movement which has been a formative influence for many of our people. We are excited by the birth and growth of churches in other lands to which our forebears gave sacrificial service. The old missionary society has gone and in its place we are part of the Council for World Mission; in this co-operative enterprise our relationships have been transformed. It is a round table at which twenty-eight churches share both needs and gifts. We seek to make a full contribution – in people, prayer, interest and money – and increasingly to receive talents and insights from others.

9.5 Confessional families. Generally speaking, people in the URC place little emphasis on our membership in confessional groups. This is partly because the bodies in which we are involved – the World Alliance of Reformed Churches and the Disciples Ecumenical Council – are consultative and unobtrusive, and partly because, as a united church we are not fully a part of any one confessional group. But we delight in fraternal links with churches in many parts of the world; with several we exchange ministers.

10. Triumphant and Struggling

We have confidence in the fellowship of the whole people of God, those, in the words of the epistle to the Hebrews, who now run the race and those who are now spectators and who surround us with their love. All find life in Christ. He is the power for new creation who binds us to God and to one another, who sets before the world a new possibility, who claims our commitment and our thankfulness. Why God is so patient with the church when it stumbles so often in the race, wanders from the way, disputes the truth and is divided at the holy table, that is a mystery. We can only offer ourselves as people whom the Spirit has moved to love the Lord.

Wesleyan Holiness Church

Members: 3,100   *Ministers: 9*   *Churches: 19*

In your tradition and experience how do you understand the nature and purpose of your church (or churches when the national body is a federation of local churches):

"We believe that the Christian church is the entire body of believers in Jesus Christ, who is the founder and only Head of the church. The church includes both those believers who have gone to be with the Lord and those who remain on the earth, having renounced the world, the flesh, and the devil, and having dedicated themselves to the work which Christ committed unto His church until He comes. The Church on earth is to preach the pure Word of God, properly administer the sacraments according to Christ's instructions, and live in obedience to all that Christ commands. A local church is a body of believers formally organized on gospel principles, meeting regularly for the purposes of evangelism, nurture, fellowship and worship. The Wesleyan Church is a denomination consisting of those members within district conferences and local churches who as members of the body of Christ hold the faith set forth in these Articles of Religion and acknowledge the ecclesiastical authority of its governing bodies. (See Matt. 16:18; 18:17; Acts 2:41-47; 11:22; I Cor. 1:2; 12:28; Gal. 1:2)."

...in relation to other Christian denominations:

"In order that we may wisely preserve and pass on to posterity the heritage of doctrine and principles of Christian living transmitted to us as evangelicals in the Arminian-Wesleyan tradition, and to insure church order by sound principles of ecclesiastical polity and to prepare the way for more effective co-operation with other branches of the church of Christ in all that makes for the advancement of God's kingdom among men, we, the ministers and lay members of The Wesleyan Church meeting in official assemblies, do herby ordain, establish, and set forth as the fundamental law, or constitution of The Wesleyan Church the articles of religion, rules of Christian living, privileges and conditions of church member-ship, and articles of organization and government."

...and as we share in God's mission to the world?

"The Wesleyan Church has grown out of a revival movement which has historically given itself to one mission – the spreading of scriptural holiness throughout every land. The message which ignited the Wesleyan revival was the announcement that God through Christ can forgive man of his sins, transform him, free him from inbred sin, enable him to live a holy life, and bear witness to his heart that he is indeed a child of God. The message was based on the Scriptures, was verified in personal experience, and came not only in word but in the power of the Spirit. It was dynamic and contagious, and was communicated from heart to heart and from land to land. It adapted itself to and gave new vitality and purpose to various kinds of church organizations."

Church of Scotland

Members: 900,000   *Ministers: 1,450*   *Churches: 1,785*

Preface

This document is offered with acknowledgement of its limits. It draws mainly on classic and other already existing statements of the Church of Scotland's self-understanding, quoting, summarising or otherwise reflecting them, and setting them in an historical and structural framework. Inevitably therefore its perspective tends to be traditional and formal. Reference will be made at the end of the document to some implications of these limitations.

1. Classic Statements of Its Self-Understanding

Article I of the Article Declaratory of the Constitution of the Church of Scotland in Matters Spiritual, declared lawful by the Church in 1921 and by Parliament in 1926

'The Church of Scotland is part of the Holy Catholic Church; worshipping one God, Almighty, all-wise and all-loving in the Trinity of the Father, the Son, and the Holy Ghost, the same in substance, equal in power and glory; adoring the Father, infinite in Majesty, of whom are all things; confessing our Lord Jesus Christ, the Eternal Son, made very man for our salvation; glorifying in His Cross and Resurrection, and owing obedience to Him as the head over all things to His Church; trusting in the promised renewal and guidance of the Holy Spirit; proclaiming the forgiveness of sins and acceptance with God through faith in Christ and the gift of Eternal life; and labouring for the advancement of the Kingdom of God throughout the world. The Church of Scotland adheres to the Scottish Reformation; receives the word of God which is contained in the Scriptures of the Old and New Testaments as its supreme rule of faith and life; and avows the fundamental doctrines of the Catholic faith founded thereupon.'

Preamble at Ordination and Induction of a Minister

'The Church of Scotland, as part of the Holy Catholic or Universal Church worshipping one God – Father, Son, and Holy Spirit – affirms anew its belief in the Gospel of the sovereign grace and love of God, wherein through Jesus Christ, His Only Son, our Lord, Incarnate, Crucified, and Risen, He freely offers to all men, upon repentance and faith, the forgiveness of sins, renewal by the Holy Spirit, and eternal life, and calls them to labour in the fellowship of faith for the advancement of the Kingdom of God throughout the world.'

2. Its Historical and Structural Background

A recent statement prepared for the Ninth Assembly of the Conference of European Churches may be summarised as follows.

The Christian church in Scotland dates at least from the beginning of the 5th century, with Celtic missionary activity which culminated in the Columban mission in mid 6th century; there may indeed have been earlier conversions in the area occupied and influenced by the Romans. The Celtic church pattern, which was influenced by Byzantium and independent of Roman jurisdiction, continued for the remaining half of the first millenium. Conformity with Rome came in the 11th century under King Malcolm III and Queen Margaret, was strengthened further by the large number of Norman landowners settled in the country by the Crown, and continued for the first half of the second millenium.

In these centuries, as elsewhere in mediaeval Europe, there were developments of the hierarchy, the parochial system and the religious houses. In this period Scotland's main links were with France, England being a common enemy. Scots were influenced by their participation in the Council of Basle in the 15th century, and the primary reforming influences in Scotland in this and the subsequent century were the conciliar movement, Hus, Luther, Zwingli and, above all, Calvin. The Reformation culminated in its legal establishment in 1560. In the 17th century, following the union of the Crowns of Scotland and England in 1603, attempts to conform the Church of Scotland forcibly to the Church of England, particularly the latter's hierarchical structure and its subservience to the Crown, led to conflict and persecution, ending in 1690 with the Revolution Settlement establishing the reformed church in its presbyterian form as the national church of Scotland.

From mid 17th to mid 18th century there was considerable controversy and schism in the church, much of it focused on the church's relations with the civil authority; the largest 'Disruption' was in 1843, when nearly a third of the Church seceded over freedom from civil intervention in the appointment of ministers. Since then most of those schisms have been healed, the majority of each of the separate reformed churches being now reunited, following a large reunion in 1900 and the largest in 1929. At each of the major settlements there was a minority which did not accept it: at the Reformation in 1560 some in outlying areas adhered to Rome; at the Revolution Settlement in 1690 some adhered to the episcopalian rather than presbyterian form; at the 1900 union some continued as the Free Church of Scotland, and at the 1929 union some continued as the United Free Church of Scotland.

The Roman Catholic Church has grown considerably through 19th and 20th century Irish immigration, and the Scottish Episcopal Church has grown to some extent through English immigration. Over the last centuries successively the Congregational, Baptist, Methodist, Disciple and Pentecostal traditions have led to further formation of congregations. A recent estimate puts the adult membership of the Church of Scotland at around 900,000, of the Roman Catholic Church at around 6/700,000, and of the other churches at around 100,000.

Accounts of theological influence in the course of history are inevitably selective and controversial. They have included – the ancient Celtic tradition with its evangelical piety and cosmic mysticism; the 16th century Reformation, especially the French reformers, Calvin and Beza, and the Swiss reformers, Bullinger and Zwingli; the 17th century Dutch neo-Calvinists and the English Puritans; the 18th century Scottish Enlightenment; the 19th and 20th century German theologians, many of whose writings were translated into English by Scottish ministers, the last major example being Karl Barth.

Throughout the centuries, at least since the Reformation, there has been fruitful tension between the more 'conservative' and the more 'liberal' theological tendencies within the Church, expressed since mid 18th century as the distinction between 'Evangelicals' and 'Moderates', and reflected in changing forms and understandings of confession of faith. The 16th century Scots Confession and Heidelberg Confession came to be overshadowed by the 17th century Westminister Confession, which in turn was challenged in the following two centuries, until a late 19th century 'conscience clause' effectively reduced its doctrinal status, though it remains the Church's 'subordinate standard'. In this Church, which contains a considerable variety of theological interpretation, there is continuing debate on the extent of tolerable diversity and on the precise way in which confessional standards influence belief.

The polity of the Church is conciliar, with councils or 'courts' (the term not being restricted to its judicial sense) appropriate to each geo-political level. The main lines of this polity were set during the period from 1560 to 1690, though not without controversy. At certain times in that period it incorporated individual episcopate by bishops alongside the corporate episcopate of councils; this episcopal element in the system was at least in part a matter of Crown imposition, appointment and control, and was excluded in 1690. The original documents provide for councils, courts, assemblies at five levels – for the parish a kirk session, for the district a presbytery, for the region a synod, for the nation a general assembly, and for the world an ecumenical council, it being recognised that in the worldwide division of the church of the time there was little immediate prospect of the convening of an oecumenical council. Kirk sessions, which oversee the local congregation and its parish, consist of elders under the presidency of a minister. There is one elder for roughly twenty members, and most are responsible for a sub-area of the parish. Presbyteries consist of all the ministers and an equal number of elders. Synods consist of a proportion of ministers and an equal number of elders representative of all the Presbyteries in the region. The annually meeting General Assembly consists of around 600 ministers and 600 elders, all representative of the Presbyteries, with all ministers attending once every four years. Each of these courts has developed committees, which may include other members of the Church, and those at national level now employ full-time staff.

Forms of worship are based on ancient catholic tradition, given formative shape in the Genevan Service Book of 1556 and the Westminster Directory of Public Worship of 1645, and incorporated in the Book of Common Order, the most recent editions of which are those of 1940 and 1979. This Common Order is a guide and not a fixed liturgy, and deliberately leaves much room for extemporary prayer. The eucharist, normally called Lord's Supper or Holy Communion, is usually celebrated less often than weekly, at either monthly or quarterly intervals, though the weekly communion which the Reformers sought to restore is now on the increase. The more frequent form of Sunday worship consists of prayers, scripture readings, sermon and singing.

The terms of church-state relations, orginally expressed theologically by the 16th century Reformers, were more fully formulated by the Church and acknowledged legislatively by Parliament this century in the Articles Declaratory, in particular Articles XV and VI (see Appendix). In this relationship of mutual recognition, the Church is free from the State but recognised by it and acknowledged to have territorial responsibility. The relationship is symbolised in the presence at every annual General Assembly of an observer sent by the Sovereign, who brings the greetings of the Crown but cannot participate in the proceedings.

3. Recent Statements of Self-Understanding

The Church has been led to define its nature and purpose in the last decade or so, stimulated on the one hand by awareness of major social change and on the other by encounter with other churches, in particular the Roman Catholic Church. Awareness of social change led it to set up a special 'Committee of Forty' to enquire into God's purpose for his people in Scotland today, and one consequence of its work was the establishment of an Assembly Council, charged among other things with the setting of priorities. Developing relations with the Roman Catholic Church led to the formation of a Joint Commission of Doctrine between the two Churches.

From Committee of Forty

The Committe of Forty in its report in 1973 on 'God's Purpose for His People in Scotland' said, among other things:

'God's purpose for His people in Scotland is what it always was and always will be. He wants us to know Him and to enjoy His company, to lead the fullest possible kind of life, this side of death and the other side of it too. That means also knowing and loving our family and neighbours.... sharing the fullest possible kind of life with them. He wants that equally for everyone,... but he has a particular care and concern for everyone who is any kind of trouble. He wants justice, peace and love, and He wants the whole human race to be gathered into His kingdom.

God's purpose for His people in Scotland is what it always was and always will be. But it is always also something new. There is still good news, and it is that God has altogether new things in store for us all.... To believe that God does not have new Things for His people to do and see and understand and obey is to go clean against what the Bible has to say about Him. There is still good news in that sense too.'

From Assembly Council

The Assembly Council in a report in 1984 said, among other things:

'We can let the Holy Spirit weave new patterns of Church life, because we believe that:

The Church is a worldwide fellowship of enormously exciting proportions, in which we share and care for one another, and in which at the present time we have probably more to learn than to give.

The Church is fragmented denominationally, but we belong essentially together and therefore must find ways of doing and being together far beyond the present conciliar patterns.

The Church is a fellowship in which men, women and children, journeying in faith, are fed by Word and Sacrament.

The worship of God in the Church is immensely exciting and joyful, because it is an echo of the worship of heaven and we are all invited, the whole people, to share in it. The Sacraments and the Word are both central, and both belong to the whole people.

The witness of the Church in the world is primarily the attractive power of the Cross and Resurrection as reflected in the lives, suffering or joyful, personal or corporate, of all its members.

The service of the Church is caring for all in need, whatever their nationality, faith, or circumstance.

The Church is nerved to do the impossible by the presence and power of the Holy Spirit. To recover our nerve we have to put ourselves in the place to receive His guidance and power.

The task of the Church is nothing less than to be the agent of Jesus Christ in the redemption of the whole creation. At certain times in history she may act as a powerful institution, at others as yeast working secretly. At all times her calling is the healing of the whole of society.'

The same Assembly Council also offered this judgement:

'The laity of the Church allow themselves to be led.

The Church is static rather than dynamic, existing for itself and for the nurture of its members rather than for the world beyond.

The Church's concern is for its own purity and life rather than the salvation of the world.'

From Joint Commission on Doctrine

The first Interim Common Report of the Joint Commission of Doctrine (Church of Scotland/Roman Catholic), presented in

1983, was precisely on 'The Doctrine of the Church'. It may be summarised as follows.

The Church of Scotland members of the Joint Commission were fully in agreement with their Roman Catholic colleagues that the church is the Body of Christ, existing with Christ at the meeting-point of the visible and the invisible, of experience and faith. Vertically incorporated by the Holy Spirit into union and communion with Jesus Christ, the church's being is a "mystery". Her character as one, holy and universal is that of Christ himself, and hence the object of faith and hope rather than sight; and it is he himself who has chosen and called her, through the Apostles. This in turn means mission on the horizontal: the people of God sent into the world visibly to embody there the presence of Christ, upbuilding his community of love, and faithfully proclaiming his gospel in word, sacrament and service. Living 'between the times', this imperfect, pilgrim people seek by the power of the Spirit to grow into and complete that oneness, holiness, catholicity and apostolic faithfulness, which are already their promise and reality in Christ.

Given this mutual understanding of the church's nature, with its unresolvable tension between the divine and the human, the vertical and the horizontal, the spiritual and the structural, the Church of Scotland members feel in principle very receptive to some of the major ecclesiological developments of Vatican II. That applies especially to the description of the church as "the universal sacrament of salvation". This affirms that the church so shares in the reality of Christ as to be a "sacrament" of his grace, both a sign and a seed of unity, hope and redemption for the whole human race. Her function, on this understanding, is to mediate to the world that salvation of which her own manifest, but imperfect, love and unity are a foretaste. Despite the unfamiliarity of the language of sacramentality as applied to the church, it is possible to acknowledge and welcome its intentions, from a Reformed point of view. To the extent that both Roman Catholic and Calvinist theologians can today speak of Christ as "the one true sacrament", the concept of the sacramentality of the church can be interpreted Christologically, as securing the Lordship of Christ himself over both the church and her sacraments.

Furthermore, it is helpful for the Reformed Churches to be reminded, by means of the concept of the sacramentality of the church, of the importance of the sacraments for their own ecclesiology. When the sacraments are neglected or subordinated, in ecclesiology or church practice, we do an injustice to our tradition and historical origins. For there Word and Sacrament are inseparably linked in mutual witness – the gospel words made visible, and the signs of the kingdom audible. In the sacraments especially the corporateness of Christian existence is made plain: the ingrafting and nourishment of those who are in Christ realised not in individualistic isolation but in community, and in communion with all the members of the one Body, of every time and place.

Even so, just because of the inseparability of Word and Sacrament, the Church of Scotland members, having acknowledged the relative usefulness of sacramentality as an ecclesiological concept, and the supreme importance of the sacraments for ecclesial life, would still wish to identify their distinctive, Reformed understanding of the church in terms of the Word. For God himself is eternally Word, and Scripture attests that it is by his Word that he creates and reconciles all things. Those who are brought by grace into a saving relationship with God comprise thereby a distinctive 'community of the Word'. Proclamation is normative and constitutive for the Church's being, and a mark of her visible, continuing presence in time and space. The Church, like faith itself, comes "by hearing"; and whenever his story is rehearsed, and his promises – made plain through the signs of word and element – are truly heard, then Christ himself is really present in our midst. Yet this very proclamation, the gift of Christ himself crucified and risen, also directs us outward, to the whole of humanity and to the cosmos, into every active form of cross-like, self abandoning mission in and for God's world.

This means that the saints in Christ, his holy people, are indeed pilgrims and servants, who fulfil their lives only by losing them, and express their holy separation from the world through their very acts of solidarity with it. Yet by reason of their sheer humanness, as well as their capacity for sin, God's people, the *ecclesia semper reformanda*, often betray their mission on Christ's behalf, through withdrawal from the world, and a preference for self-preservation over self-giving. This is God's risk with his church, the hazarding of his gospel and ministry of reconciliation to frail and fallible human servants. Partly through awareness of her own historical origins, the Reformed Church insists upon the precariousness of the Christian community – its potential for radical failure and faithfulness, through deafness to the demands of the Word and muteness in its proclamation. We therefore can in no way accept, with our Roman Catholic colleagues, any concept of the Church's "indefectibility" – as if human forms and structures, however filled with the Spirit, could aspire to that perfection and freedom from error which belong only to Christ himself. On the other hand, Reformed soteriology and ecclesiology themselves recognise 'the perseverance of the saints', and the *Westminster Confession of Faith* itself attests the endurance of the Church through God's own power. There is a significant overlap between God's enduring commitment to the Church, and what contemporary Roman Catholics mean by 'indefect-ibility'. Thus the Interim Common Report of the Joint Commission concludes: "inasmuch as we are all referred away from ourselves to God, whose grace is unfailing, whose Word is dependable, and who may be trusted to bless and preserve his elect unto the last, we come together, at the end, to the common, solid foundation of all Christian hope and unity: the power of God's love, and the faithfulness of his promises".

From Papal Visit Document

During the papal visit to Scotland in 1982, the Church submitted to the Pope a descriptive document, which included a section entitled 'Self-Understanding'. After quoting the preamble at Ordination and Induction, and adding that the Church treasures the Apostle's and Nicene Creeds, it defined the Church's self-understanding further by the terms Reformed, National, Missionary and Ecumenical, as follows.

Reformed

A church of the Genevan or Calvinist Reformation, it is yet conscious of its roots in, and continuity with, the pre-Reformation and New Testament Church. It is Reformed but *semper reformanda* under the word of God. A founder member of the former World Presbyterian Alliance, now the World Alliance of Reformed Churches, it treasures the traditional reformed independence of outside interference yet enjoys an unusual relationship with the State. It accepts no head except Jesus Christ, yet receives the recognition of the Crown, which is sworn to uphold the Presbyterian form of Church government in Scotland.

National

The Church of Scotlanmd is national in the sense of being "representative of the Christian faith of the Scottish people".

– in the sense of being the largest Church, with just under one million communicant members in a population of five million;

– in the sense of a certain status in relationship with the community and with local and national government;

and in the sense above all of a responsibility through the parish system for the whole country and its whole life.

Here also there are tensions to be recognised: that very representativeness may encourage a triumphalism that assumes an authority in the community; that dominance in size may encourage an assumption of leadership over other Christian bodies; that status in the community may lead to an identification with the *status quo* in society.

If such temptations are not consciously resisted, a Church may fail to witness in its own life to the Cross of Christ in it poverty and suffering.

Missionary

It is a Church therefore with an awareness of responsibility for Scotland and for mission abroad. Its long overseas missionary tradition is a response to the thrust of the Gospel. It rejoices in the new phase of mission, partnership with Churches elsewhere, especially in Africa and India. It enjoys links with expatriate Scots and others of the Reformed tradition, as in the cities of Europe, including Rome.

Ecumenical

The Church of Scotland's ecumenism is not a development of this century only, although it is itself the product of at least three Presbyterian traditions uniting in 1900 and 1929, but is also the position affirmed in its official standards in Article VII of its Articles Declaratory: "The Church of Scotland, believing it to be the will of Christ that his disciples should be all one in the Father and in Him, that the world may believe that the Father has sent Him, recognises the obligation to seek and promote union with other Churches in which it finds the Word to be purely preached, the sacraments administered according to Christ's ordinance, and discipline rightly exercised..."'

The documenet went on to suggest three points of convergence between the Church of Scotland and the Roman Catholic Church, namely the Word, Collegiality and Diversity.

4. Underlying Unities

A recurring theme in some of the above statements is of the unity that underlies distinctions, e.g. of the vertical and the horizontal, of the spiritual and the structural, of the audible word and the visible sacrament, of the church as sign of God's reign and as seed of it, of the gospel's proclamation and its manifestation.

This apparently Reformed emphasis on underlying unities has also emerged in dialogue with other traditions, such as Lutheran and Baptist; these have included the unities of – Old and New Testaments, law and gospel, creation and redemption.

A similar emphasis has been expressed in recent discussions on mission, which have drawn attention to the unity of mission and worship, of mission and ministry, and of mission and unity.

Mission and Worship

It has been said that there is a double movement between God and the world, namely mission, which is God's worldward movement, and worship, which is the world's Godward movement, and that the church is called to embody the two movements, as agent both of God's mission and of the world's worship. Thus its twin tasks are evangelical or news-giving and doxological or glory-giving. In similar vein, it has been said that the church breathes in as it gathers for worship (in congregation or *synagoge*) and breathes out as it scatters for mission (in dispersion or *diaspora*); so it is *ecclesia*, a body called out, and *apostole*, a body sent out.

Mission and Ministry

The notion, that some parts of the world or of a country are to be objects of mission and others to be objects of ministry, has been abandoned. When mission is understood as the movement of God to his world, in which in the sending of his Son he gives himself to it, and by which both individuals and communities are progressively transformed, it can no longer be equated with the more limited process by which individuals or communities come to call themselves Christian. It becomes clear that countries long called Christian, and indeed individuals so called, require mission, and that the distinction between ministry and mission dissolves. It is in line with this insight that the two formerly separate departments of the Church have been amalgamated into one department of 'Ministry and Mission'.

Mission and Unity

A similar integration has produced the unified department of 'World Mission and Unity'. The already quoted Article VII of the 1921 Articles Declaratory makes clear that unity is of the essence of the church and of the mission of God of which it is part. This bond between mission and unity is further elaborated in the 1929 Uniting Act, as follows:

'The Church of Scotland and the United Free Church of Scotland, as branches of the Holy Catholic or Universal Church, believing that it is the will of their Lord for his disciples that they all should be one, acknowledge that the witness borne to the Lord by the Catholic Visible Church and the particular Churches which are members thereof, is obscured, and that His work is hindered by division and separation therein...

...the obligation resting upon the followers of Christ to manifest their inward and spiritual unity to the world, in a common profession of faith and observance of the ordinances of Christ, has never ceased to be acknowledged by the Scottish Church throughout all her branches, so that ... separations (were) contemplated and carried through with profound reluctance and in hope of ultimate reunion...

...these Churches deeply conscious of the evils of disunion, and being increasingly impressed with the urgent need for reunion in order to meet more adequately the religious requirements of the people..welcomed the opportunity...to confer together on the formation of a Basis of Union."

This commitment to 'ane face of kirk' can be traced back to the unquestioned assumption of the Reformers that there is only one church. The very vehemence of the strife especially of the 17th and 18th centuries is testimony to that conviction. The controversies were heated, because it was the common life of the one family that was at stake and not the provision of a choice of brands in a market of private religions. Such relaxed and laissez-faire denominational pluralism was a later North American development. Nor has there been any direct counterpart to the English tradition of Dissent, as a kind of religious version of Her Majesty's Opposition. The assumption has been that in every land there should be one church.

Particular and Universal

That the church is both 'catholic' and 'particular' has always been part of the Church's self-understanding. It has differed from some other churches in locating the main 'particular' church at the level of the nation rather than the diocese or the neighbourhood. It has placed this emphasis on the 'national church', because the nation, as civil community, with its combination of social, cultural, economic and political elements, is highly constitutive of human life and is therefore a prime object of redemption; indeed the Church has considered the civil authority as well as itself to be an agent of redemption of the civil community, as is expounded in Article VI of the Article Declaratory; in this it parts company with the individualist theology of modern privatised culture. However, this emphasis on the 'church national' has always been accompanied officially by a belief in the 'church universal'. The Calvinist emphasis on God's sovereign and free grace has always contained the conviction that grace, being unconditional, is also universal and encompasses the human and cosmic totality, or oikoumene.

It must be acknowledged however that the national emphasis has at times overshadowed the universal. So it was not without difficulty that at the end of the 18th century the Church was persuaded to engage in mission in Asia and elswhere in the 'whole inhabited earth', or oikoumene. But it *was* persuaded, and today its partnership with churches in Asia, Africa, the Caribbean and elsewhere, and its membership of the World Council of Churches will not allow it to forget that it belongs to a worldwide community transcending all human divisions, and that, as its first Article declares, it is 'part of the Holy Catholic or Universal church'.

5. Finally

It must be acknowledged, as was indicated in the Preface, that since the above is largely derived from already formulated documents, it does not adequately reflect either the self-understanding of the great mass of Christian people who are never involved in preparing such documents or the great development in the contemporary world and church which are so immediate and encompassing in their effects that they cannot yet be formulated in documents. Missing therefore are many of the simplicities and subtleties, and much of the range, depth and power of insight, of so-called 'ordinary' Christian experience. Missing also are the effects on the Church's self-understanding of its most recent encounters with the wider world. There is its encounter, through sociological surveys, specialised chaplaincies and pioneering movements like the Iona Community, with the wider world of Scotland itself, in which it is recognising the extent of the passing of Christendon and is facing a public which increasingly questions its claims. Above all there is its encounter with the wider world church, from which it is learning that the 'one holy catholic church' of which it is part comprehends many Christian traditions of which the Western European tradition, both Catholic and Reformed, is only one, and most significantly of all, that the main weight of the Christian community is now in the Southern hemisphere. It is therefore realising that a church which is Scottish and Reformed has more to receive than to give.

The Committe of Forty had this to say:
'The whole witness of the Bible points to a God who calls His people out and on from where they are, not knowing where they are to go, and the true image of the Church is of the community of the future and not of the past. Exodus, exile, dispersion, pilgrimage – this is the life of the people of God. The problems and decisions they pose take new forms, but a lack of settled quiet is no new experience for the Church. It is our tradition that we have been able to change, sometimes quite radically, yet still retain our identity and our sense of calling and purpose as God's people.'

APPENDIX ON CHURCH-STATE RELATIONS

Articles IV and VI of the Articles Declaratory

IV. This Church, as part of the Universal Church wherein the Lord Jesus Christ has appointed a government in the hands of Church office-bearers, receives from Him, its Divine King and Head, and from Him alone, the right and power subject to no civil authority to legislate, and to adjudicate finally, in all matters of doctrine, worship, government, and discipline in the Church, including the right to determine all questions concerning memberships and office in the Church, the constitution and membership of its Courts, and the mode of election of its office-bearers, and to define the boundaries of the sphere of labour of its ministers and ofice-bearers. Recognition by civil authority of the separate and independent government and jurisdiction of this Church in matters spiritual, in whatever manner such recognition be expressed, does not in any way affect the character of this government and jurisdiction as derived from the Divine Head of the Church alone, or give to the civil authority any right of interference with the proceedings or judgements of the Church within the sphere of its spiritual government and jurisdiction.

VI. This Church acknowledges the divine appointment and authority of the civil magistrate within his own sphere, and maintains its historic testimony to the duty of the nation acting in its corporate capacity to render homage to God, to acknowledge the Lord Jesus Christ to be King over the nations, to obey His laws, to reverence His ordinances, to honour His Church, and to promote in all appropriate ways the Kingdom of God. The Church and State owe mutual duties to each other, and acting within their respective spheres may signally promote each other's welfare. The Church and the State have the right to determine each for itself all questions concerning the extent and the continuance of their mutual relations in the discharge of these duties and obligations arising therefrom.

Congregational Union of Scotland

Members: 21,000   *Ministers: 85*   *Churches: 99*

Over the past twenty years, there have been two significant changes in Scottish Congregationalism in relation to other denominations. First, there has been a definite move from the periphery to the centre in our Church-life. This can be seen in a number of ways – the acceptance of central decisions about stipend and pensions, the willingness to have the Union speak and act in the name of the whole denomination, the erosion of District Councils and the greater prominence given to our Annual Assembly, the greater emphasis on the central control on recruitment and training for lay and ordained ministries. The result is that we are now ready to discuss objectively the central payment of ministers and the possibility of the Union becoming a church. There are those who see all this as, in part at least, us making adjustments in our internal life prior to union with more 'structured' Churches cf. The experience of Congregationalists in England moving from a Union to a Church before the formation of the United Reformed Church in 1972. Second, there has been a growing willingness to consider Church union. While nothing came of discussions with the Church of Scotland, the Churches of Christ and the United Free Church, while we cannot be sure of the outcome of the Multilateral Conversations or our talks with the United Reformed Church, the momentum for union is certainly growing. The lobby of those who resisted all mention, far less consideration, of Church unity has become smaller and weaker over the years. Now the questions are "when"? and "how?" rather than "why?"

As far as sharing in God's mission in the world is concerned, the formation of the Council for World Mission and its work over the years has effected two further changes in our Church-life. First, we realise that we must work with God in His mission locally, the

Church is to be, represent and proclaim His good news in its own setting. The mistaken notion that mission was our sending God and His news into another context in another country on another continent is in its death-throes. Second, we see mission as that activity of the Church in which all Churches share. There are no boundaries to mission because mission is not acting in God's name, on His behalf, but co-operating with God wherever He is at work i.e. the world is our parish. And that statement is true for every Church, in First and Third worlds, in city and in country, down-town and suburban, rich and poor.

John W. S. Clark,
November 1985

Scottish Episcopal Church

Members: 38,000   Ministers: 235   Churches: 305

**"In your tradition and experience, how do you understand
the nature and purpose of your Church
(1) in relation to other Christian Denominations and
(2) as we share in God's mission to the world?"**

The answer to this question in the space of not more that 4/5 A4's must inevitably be indicative, not definitive, expressing not every view and understanding, but a general consensus.

The Scottish Episcopal Church is part of historic Scottish Christianity which, largely through accidents of political history, now includes in its membership a very small proportion of the Scottish population. But numerical size is not the most significant factor. The Episcopal Church has always had a self-awareness as a Church, and this has been immensely reinforced and strengthened as a result of the world–wide development of the Anglican Communion. Our Scottishness gives us our historical identity; Anglicanism saves us from becoming inward–looking either in our theology or our nationalist attitudes. To be Anglicans is to be part of a world–wide communion which is developing its sense of inter-dependence, province to province, around the world.

To express, then, our understanding of our nature, it is necessary to say something about the Anglican Communion. The Anglican Tradition in fact predates the Reformation of the 16th Century. Perhaps its roots are to be found in what we now know as the Renaissance, of which the Reformation itself is a consequence; it represents a particular response to both these movements. It thinks of itself as being at once Catholic and Reformed, and as holding, in a particular balance and tension, the centrality of scripture, tradition and reason. But Anglicanism sees its roots not simply in the Renaissance and the reformation: the particular temper or mood it represents goes back, it believes, to the patristic period. In the Episcopal Church, this awareness is perhaps most clearly and particularly expressed through its liturgical worship, which, even today, continues to attract many.

The Episcopal Church, like every Church in the United Kingdom, has undergone enormous changes in the last quarter of a century, and these changes have introduced many strains and conflicts among us. Our motto is "Evangelical Truth and Apostolic Order" and as long as that motto is interpreted in terms of aspiration rather than of description, it is acceptable; but in our past we have perhaps placed at least as much emphasis on our possession of "apostolic order" in the three-fold ministry of bishops, priests and deacons, as we have on "evangelical truth", and we are certainly sensitive to the criticisms that we had become little more than an Episcopalian sect. With the development of the ecumenical movement, great changes have taken place, not only in our relationships with other Churches (whether Roman Catholic or Presbyterian), but changes also in our understanding of what 'apostolic order' means. An element in the tradition and practice of our Church which we value highly, yet which we feel is not always adequately appreciated by others, is the role of lay people in congregation, diocese and Province; pastorally, liturgically, administratively and, together with Bishops and presbyters in the General Synod, in the determination of matters of faith and morals. The ecumenical movement in Scotland has a history of failed 'schemes', but the development of world-wide ecumenical documents like BEM, ARCIC, Anglican/Reformed, Anglican/Orthodox, Anglican/Lutheran, have set our own traditional attitudes in a much wider context. In addition to inter-Church co-operation which takes place at the local level, often patchily and sometimes sporadically, there are in Scotland two formally recognised Local Ecumenical Projects – one in Livingston and the other in central Edinburgh. It is the experience of most of our clergy and lay people that the initiative in ecumenical co-operation is often taken by the Scottish Episcopal Church.

We have spoken of our awareness of being part of a larger whole: but this has in itself been a cause of anxiety.

"Once there was something called the Scottish Episcopal Church: now there is just a Province of the Anglican Communion. Yet it is our membership of the Anglican Communion with its increasingly effective network of communication which gives us a renewed significance in the Scottish church scene and provides insights beyond our own resources."

Loss of such traditional self-awareness is still a threat to some; when a very small body faces very large bodies like the Church of Scotland or Scottish Roman Catholicism, the fear of absorption without trace cannot be entirely ignored. One of the criticisms of the Episcopal Church was summed up by a distinguished Scottish elder when he described us in a T.V. interview as "un-Scottish, un-Reformed, and toffee-nosed". The first of these is historical nonsense; the second depends upon what you mean by "Reformed" – we don't claim to be Presbyterian; the third is the sting in the tail – there is no doubt that the Episcopal Church has a higher proportion of middle and upper class members than other Scottish Churches. Part of the difficulty we face in our home mission work, lies in the feeling among many Scots that to become an Episcopalian is to deny one's authentic Scottish culture. The Episcopal Church owes a great deal to many years of faithful service by many furth of Scotland, both clergy and laity.

In its missionary outreach, whether at home or overseas, whether in evangelism, social service or education, the Episcopal Church has often felt like a very small ship trying to carry much too large a sail. Our reach almost invariably exceeds our grasp.

Once Overseas missionary work meant *'Kaffraria'* in South Africa and *'Chanda'* in India, but now our awareness of universal belonging has widened and diversified our co-operation, both with Anglican missionary societies and with overseas dioceses. Ironically, however, this wider vision has reduced our sense of personal relationship and responsibility to the Church overseas; there is then the danger of relationships becoming confined to occasional visits overseas by us, or to our welcoming visitors from overseas, and, to the transfer of funds by us. The financing of an Overseas Ordinand in our Theological College is a small step towards modifying this danger.

In Home Mission work, our 'success' has often been sociologically determined. We are more likely to succeed in establishing a congregation in a white-collar suburb than in an area of multiple deprivation. The positive side of this is that such a membership gives the Episcopal Church the opportunity to exercise an influence in society and engage effectively with the social and political issues rather than simply seek to nurture its own members. The negative aspect is that we find it difficult to provide the kind of worshipping life or church activities within which others feel at home. Although in the last century notable ministries like that of Bishop Forbes in Dundee did bridge the gap between rich and poor, we find it increasingly difficult to sustain congregations in areas of urban deprivation. Nevertheless we have quite deliberately not withdrawn from such areas, recognising that we need to be involved in them for our own souls' health, as much as for any contribution we can make to them. Where possible, of course, we look for ecumenical co-operation in home mission work, but it must be confessed that in this regard realisation frequently falls short of desire.

In our education work we concentrate on "equipping God's people for their work of ministry". This includes training and in-service training of the clergy, and training for non-stipendiary ministry of men and women, both ordained and lay; the nurturing of children, young people and adults in their understanding of the faith, and their personal and congregational life and witness. Our Theological College is closely related to the Faculty of Divinity in Edinburgh University, and plays a very significant role in our Church's life, not least in our ecumenical relationships.

In social responsibility, the role of our Church in social and political issues is not seen, by some of our membership, as integral to our work of mission: for others, there is an acceptable Christian political involvement, which sets criteria for discussion, but remains aloof from decision-making processes; for yet others, there can be, in certain circumstances and on certain issues, a legitimate campaigning stance, integral to a prophetic theology. Alongside this internal discussion, there is the practical question of resources. We are a small body, and put almost the whole of our manpower and money into maintaining a parochial structure which seeks to cover the whole of Scotland. Anything which is undertaken beyond that has to be done either by the voluntary efforts of lay people, or by the clergy who undertake provincial responsibilities. Consequently, there is a danger that people will either be overstretched, or that work undertaken will be inadequately prepared and carried out.

In spite of these difficulties however, our Church has moved in the past few years from the traditional support of a home for unmarried mothers, with an adoption and social work agency, to, for example, a social service unit in the diocese of Glasgow serving an area of multiple deprivation, and to an increasing desire to be a presence in the inner-city urban areas in our major towns. There is also a 'Peace Project' funded by our Church, to work with all sides in the peace debate, in the hope of achieving better understanding, based on knowledge of the facts of the situation, and an awareness of the fears which polarise opinion. Finally, a family work project, 'Bringing Up Parents' is currently exploring the nature of the Christian family, and we continue to run two homes for the elderly.

In all this, of course, we recognise that, quite apart from theological conviction, a Church like ours can function effectively in social responsibility only if we co-operate ecumenically with others; though, from experience, it must be added that greater co-operation can often be achieved in small-scale, local tasks than when we, with other Churches in Scotland, seek to co-operate nationally: winning the approval of several different kinds of authorising bodies can frustrate the best of intentions!

To sum up – at one time there were those who thought that the mission of the Episcopal Church was to convert all Scots, including Roman Catholics, and Presbyterians, and all the rest to Episcopalianism! Few would support that view today. Perhaps it would be truer to say that the Episcopal Church sees itself in Scotland very much as the Anglican Communion sees itself in the world: – not as The Church in any exclusive sense, but as a Church which, in the mercy and providence of God, has received and developed, lived by and witnessed to, a particular tradition, which is both catholic and reformed, and which seeks, by a balance of scripture, tradition and reason, to interpret the unchanging gospel to the changing social, political and cultural contexts of our world; committed to seeking unity with other churches; receiving much from them, but also contributing a little to them; rather like a trace element in the soil, in itself of no significant size, but one whose presence is necessary to health and productivity.

★ Edward Brechin
Primus Convenor, Faith and Order Board
January, 1986.

Roman Catholic Church in Scotland

Members: 360,000   *Ministers: 1,145*   *Churches: 620*

At Bellahouston, on the occasion of the Pope's visit to Scotland in the Summer of 1982, the Catholic community both sensed and celebrated its identity. It was Scots, identifying with the country and people of Scotland, and with their history. Catholics of this generation were united in faith with such forebears as Ninian and Columba, Margaret and John Ogilvie. The Celtic, Medieval and Counter-reformation churchmen and women were one with them in the long annuals of the Christian faith in Scotland.

At the same time the presence of bishops from neighbouring countries, and indeed of many Scots of Irish, English and continental European backgrounds, reflected the universality of the Catholic Church, and gave expression, in an easily assimilated way, to the reality of the Catholic Church as a communion of Churches, historically and geographically distinct, but united in one faith, by one sacramental ministry, and in a common experience of community. The presence of the Holy Father, as the leader on earth of this communion, and the visible centre of its unity, confirmed and crowned this Catholic sense of Church.

The Pope caught the flavour and challenge of that time of grace when he said:

> *"You originate in a glorious past, but you do not live in the past. You belong to the present and your generation must not be content simply to rest on the laurels won by your grandparents and great-grandparents. You must give your response to Christ's call to follow him and enter with him as co-heirs into his Father's heavenly Kingdom".* [1]

The Pope identified as one of those responses, called forth

by our times, ecumenical endeavour. At the end of his discourse, in words which have since become legendary in Scotland, Pope John Paul addressed ALL Scottish Christians as his beloved brethren in Christ, and invited them to make their pilgrimage "together hand-in-hand".[2]

Scottish Catholics, conscious of their heritage and proud of their identity, are more than ready to co-operate with other Christian communities in Scotland in the quest for the unity for which Christ prayed, and to join this inter-Church process with the humbling and yet challenging awareness that indeed "we are not strangers but pilgrims".

The following submission is divided into two parts.
In the first, on **THE NATURE AND PURPOSE OF THE CHURCH**, we look at the Catholic Church as it is in itself, in the light of its classical ecclesiology as formulated anew by the Second Vatican Council and other recent documents.
We examine it briefly under the following headings:
1. The Church as MYSTERY.
2. The Church as COMMUNION.
3. The Church as SACRAMENT.
4. The Church HIERARCHICALLY constituted.
5. The Church endowed with SPIRITUAL GIFTS.
6. The PILGRIM Church.
7. The MISSION of the Church.

In the second part we look at
THE RELATIONSHIP OF THE ROMAN CATHOLIC CHURCH TO OTHER CHRISTIAN CHURCHES AND COMMUNITIES.
It is natural that we should see this relationship first in respect of other Christian Churches in Scotland, before proceeding to a brief examination of some important aspects of the relationship of the Catholic Church to other Churches in general, and which qualify the dialogue betwen us:

1. The Catholic Church and CHRISTIAN UNITY.
2. The ONE Church.
3. The Church in PARTIAL COMMUNION with others.

I. The Nature and Purpose of the Church

1. The Church as Mystery.

Vatican II approached the nature of the Church through the biblical concept of 'mystery'. In St. Paul, the mystery is the plan of salvation hidden in God from before all ages, prepared in the history of Israel, revealed and fulfilled in Christ, and proclaimed to the nations by the Church.[3]

So when we speak of the mystery of the Church, we mean that the Church exists from and for God's gracious plan of salvation. We mean that the Church is a people called into being by the Holy Trinity. The Church originates in the free purpose of God the Father to communicate his love through his Son and in the power of the Holy Spirit to men and women of all generations.

As mystery the Church is the creation of God the Father. As mystery the Church is the Body of Christ. As mystery the Church is indeed filled with the presence of the Holy Spirit.

As mystery the Church can never be reduced to the level of religious phenomenon. It is mystery, the covenanted sphere of God's operation in the world. In his Spirit Jesus Christ is always present in the Church as its risen Lord. This presence of the Risen Lord directs the People of God towards their final end:
"The eschatological character of the Church is clearly evident from its relation to Christ. Thus, the pilgrim Church on earth is a messianic people, which is already in itself an anticipation of the new creation. However, the Church continues to include sinners among its members, for it is both holy and in need of purification as it journeys on through the persecutions of the world and the consolations of God towards the kingdom which is yet to come. Thus, the mystery of the Cross and the mystery of the Resurrection are always present together in the Church."[4]

2. The Church as Communion

This Church exists in history as the new People of God and is constituted by all those who believe in Christ and who are baptised with water and the Holy Spirit.

The heart of the Church's life is the communion of this People of God, communion with God and among the members through Jesus Christ and in the Holy Spirit. "Communion is a profound inner principle of the life of the Church. It points to the mystery of grace which lies at the heart of the Church...It speaks of community and relationship and harmony within the Body of Christ."[5]

3. The Church as Sacrament

The recent Synod of Bishops reflected on the sources of this ecclesial communion and drew attention especially to its sacramental dimension: "This communion exists through the Word of God and the sacraments. Baptism is the door to the Church's communion and its foundation. The eucharist is the source of the entire Christian life and its summit. Communion with the Body of Christ in the eucharist signifies and accomplishes, or builds up, the initmate union of all the faithful in the Body of Christ which is the Church."[6]

4. The Church Hierarchically Constituted

This communion of the People of God also has what is called a HIERARCHICAL dimension: we believe that the ministry of the apostles is perpetuated in the Church by the College of bishops which has the Pope, the successor of Peter, as its head. The bishops in turn are part of an ecclesiastical, or ecclesial, ministry, considered as essential to the Church, and which "is exercised in different degrees by those who even from ancient times have been called bishops, priests and decons."[7]

5. The Church Endowed with Spiritual Gifts

The Church is also filled with the many gifts, charisms, services and ministries which the Holy Spirit arouses and bestows within God's People. Furthermore "all the baptised according to their gifts are responsible for the well-being and growth of the unity and communion of the Church...Through their baptism and confirmation the faithful are fully qualified to promote the mission of the Church."[8]

6. The Pilgrim Church

The People of God is also a pilgrim Church. "It's destiny is the Kingdom of God which has been begun by himself on earth and which must be further extended until it is brought to perfection by him at the end of time."[9]

Consequently the present state of the Church is marked by a certain incompletion and imperfection: "The Church, to which we are all called in Christ Jesus, and in which by the grace of God we acquire holiness, will receive its perfection only in the glory of heaven, when will come the time of the renewal of all things."[10]

Yet at the same time the mystery of this eschatological dimension of the Church's life is that the destiny towards which the Spirit is directing the Church is present and active in a hidden way even in the here and now. Thus the Church remains essentially one both in the time of its pilgrimage and in the time of its glorification.[11]

Christians make their pilgrimage towards the Kingdom of the Father along with men and women of all ages, nations and creeds, sharing the one history of mankind, united already in the promotion of goodness, justice, and genuine human development. Gradually the communion of the baptised opens to and is fulfilled in the perfect communion of the eschatological kingdom of God when "all the just from the time of Adam, 'from Abel the just one, to the last of the elect' will be gathered together with the Father in the universal Church."[12]

7. The Mission of the Church

The Church exists from and for God's plan of salvation for the world. Consequently, "the Church's essential mission, following that of Christ, is a mission of evangelisation and salvation."[13]

Through its preaching of God's word, through its celebration of the mysteries of salvation in the sacraments, and through its constant service to the gospel and its values, the Church is and must be the sacrament of salvation, "a sign and instrument, that is, of cummunion with God and of union among men."[14]

The Church's mission, through word, sacrament and witness, is to be a living and dynamic sign in the world of the salvation which the Father offers us in the paschal mystery of his Son Jesus Christ through the gift of the Holy Spirit.

In carrying out this mission, the Church teaches us the way we have to follow to enter the Kingdom of God. The Church guides us in Christian discipleship, true morality, a spirit of prayer and in the path to holiness.

In recent times, Christians have become increasingly aware that the Church's mission of evangelisation and salvation inescapably implies a commitment to integral human development. Christ commanded us to love one another, and "the love which impels the Church to communicate to all people a sharing in the grace of divine life also causes her, through the effective action of her members, to pursue people's temporal good, help them in their needs, provide for their education and promote an integral liberation from everything that hinders the development of individuals."[15]

By looking to these concerns, the Church, in which the kingdom of God is present in mystery, will be the servant of that kingdom as it develops and grows in this world and comes to its fullness in the world to come.

II *Relationship of the Roman Catholic Church to other Christian Churches and Communities*

The Catholic Church in Scotland numbers a minority, though a substantial one, of Scottish Christians. Especially in recent times, motivated by its Commission for Christian Unity, the Catholic Church has been partner to an increasing number of ecumenical initiatives at both local and national level, especially with the Church of Scotland and the Scottish Episcopal Church.

Together with the Catholic Church throughout the world we consider the divisions among Christians to be a serious scandal to the message of the gospel and we are totally committed to the re-creation of Christian unity.

We therefore look with pleasure, but not complacency, on any significant ecumenical progress. We note the Common Statements between ourselves and the Scottish Episcopal Church on baptism, eucharist and priesthood.[16] We also note the work being done by the Joint Commission for Doctrine between the Church of Scotland and the Roman Catholic Church in Scotland, as well as the endeavours of other ecumenical agencies.

Along with other Christians we find the Final Report of ARCIC and the Lima Document impressive, and we recommend them to the serious consideration of all Christians. These can rightly be looked upon as landmarks in recent ecumenical dialogue.

Relations between Catholic and Protestant in Scotland have not always been as peaceful as they are now. We are glad to say that much of the bigotry and bitterness has subsided, although it still lingers on in some people, places and institutions.

Instead there is a growing consciousness among people of the need to give common and concerted witness if the gospel of Christ is to be credible to the population at large. The effective joint action of Church leaders in recent years over industrial and economic matters is an eloquent case in point.

1. Christian unity
Often Christians pursue unity without clearly stating what they mean by Christian unity. While there is always an element of the unknown and the unexpected about the way in which the Spirit is moving the Churches, the Catholic Church clearly understands Christian unity as the organic unity of the Christian people in such a way that believers will be united in the profession of one faith, with the service of one ministry, and celebrating one eucharist.

In ecumenical discusion there are often different models of Church unity operating tacitly in the background. We would welcome a greater degree of clarity in this matter.

2. The Church is One

Together with other Christians, we profess the Church of Christ to be one. It is part of Catholic consciousness that this oneness of the Church of Christ is not simply something which belongs to the future of the Church, but can be found existing here and now in the Roman Catholic Church. Thus, "the sole Church of Christ...subsists in the Catholic Church, which is governed by the successor of Peter and by the bishops in communion with him."[17]

The International Theological Commission recently clarified this feature of Catholic consciousness: there are certain elements which constitute the being of the true Church of Christ: the Scriptures, the doctrine of faith, the Church's magisterium, sacraments and ministries, and continuity with Peter and the apostles which is visibly preserved. These essential elements of the visible constitution of the Church are not to be separated from its spiritual dimension. The one Church of Christ can be historically verified where these elements are to be found. Without denying that some or many of these elements may also exist outside the Catholic Church, it is part of our self-consciousness that these essential constitutive elements of the Church of Christ exist in their fullness in the Roman Catholic Church.[18]

We believe that this unity, which already characterises that communion of particular Churches which we call the Catholic Church, is intended by God to envelop all who believe in Christ. For this Christ prayed at the Last Supper. (John 17: 11-24). The Catholic Church sees it, therefore, as one of her main ecumenical tasks, to share this grace of unity, so that all may be united in faith, in ministry and sacramental communion. At the same time we recognise the graces, stemming from the same source, the action of the Holy Spirit among all believers, which other ecclesial communities, properly called Churches, enjoy, and which they have to offer to the wider community of Christians.[19]

3. The Church in Partial Communion with Others

The situation which currently characterises the relationship of our Church to other Christians is not simply one of division or separation, but one of partial communion. Through our baptism, all Christians are incorporated into Christ and this "constitutes the sacramental bond of unity existing among all who through it are reborn".[20]

The problem is to understand how all Christians can be incorporated into Christ through baptism and yet live in a situation of only partial ecclesial communion. This requires a lot of reflection and study. But the fact of the matter is that full ecclesial communion does not exist in practice. The ecumenical project must be to re-create that full ecclesial communion in faith, ministry and eucharist which would follow from our baptismal incorporation into Christ.

As time passes and ecumenical initiatives grow in number and quality, we are aware that this state of partial or imperfect communion gradually inches its way towards fuller communion in prayer, faith, mission and understanding.[21]

This is God's work and we rejoice in it.

SUBMISSION OF THE NATIONAL COMMISSION PRESIDENT OF CHRISTIAN DOCTRINE AND UNITY ON BEHALF OF THE ROMAN CATHOLIC CHURCH IN SCOTLAND TO THE INTER-CHURCH PROCESS, 'NOT STRANGERS BUT PILGRIMS'.
MAY 1986.

1. **"The Pope in Britain** – Collected homilies and Speeches". St. Paul Pub. 1982 p.76.
2. ibid. p. 79.
3. Cf. Rom 16:25; Eph. 1:9; 3:3,9; 6:19; Col. 1:27; 4:3.
4. Extraordinary Synod of Bishops, 1985: **Final Report**.
5. **Life in Communion**, Theology Commission of Scotland, 1983.
6. **Final Report.**
7. Vatican II, **Lumen Gentium**, 28.
8. **Life in Communion**, nos.5 and 8.
9. **Lumen Gentium**, 9.
10. **Lumen Gentium**, 48.
11. International Theological Commission, **Themata selecta de ecclesiologia**, no.10, 1985.

12. **Lumen Gentium**, 2
13. Congr. for Doctrine of the Faith, **Instruction on Christian Freedom and Liberation**, no.63, March 1986.
14. **Lumen Gentium**, 1
15. CDF, **Instr. on Christian Liberation and Freedom**, no.63.
16. The Nature of Baptism and its place in the life of the Church ('69) **The Ecclesial Nature of the Eucharist** (1973); **Priesthood and the Eucharist** (1979): Common Statements by the Joint Study Groups of Representatives of the Roman Catholic Church in Scotland and the Scottish Episcopal Church.
17. Vatican II, **Lumen Gentium**, 8.
18. Themata selecta de ecclesiologia, 9.2, 1985
19. Unitatis Redintegratio – Decree of II Vatican Council on Ecumenism – 1, 3.
20. Vatican II, **Decree on Ecumenism** 22.
21. Cf. French Bishops' Response to the Lima Report

Baptist Union of Wales

Members: 34,000   *Ministers: 215*   *Churches: 605*

Ourselves

Baptists came to Wales some three and a half centuries ago. A movement woven of several Reformation stands, it established itself firmly but unevenly throughout the country. Somewhat of an intruder when it first appeared it became naturalised, adopted the language of the people and thereafter its bilingualism held two cultures together in the service of Christ and His church. The structures developed to give expression to this dualism of language and feeling may seem puzzling to the uninitiated, but they have proved effective in enabling churches which value their autonomy and differing backgrounds to "keep the unity of the Spirit in the bond of peace".

Baptists cannot rejoice in that comprehension which is such a commendable feature of Anglicanism, nevertheless their fellowship is able to embrace, sometimes uneasily, a wide variety of convictions and practices. Their buildings are held on trusts which are invariably Calvinistic. Welsh Baptists generally are, or are legally expected to be, Particular Baptists, implying the limited nature of the efficacy of redemption. But most Welsh Baptists have moved away from rigid positions. They would regard themselves as evangelical in that in their baptism they make public avowal of their faith in Jesus Christ as Saviour and Lord, to whom the New Testament bears faithful witness and who through the Holy Spirit continues to be present in His church.

There have been other shifts from what were regarded once as fixed and unchangeable positions. There have been new understandings of accepted beliefs, adjustments and rein-terpretations, the discovery of lost values. Thus, for example, many Baptists are asking, 'Is not Christ with the believer in his baptism and therefore is the act of baptism not more than self-offering and dedication? And does not Christ preside at His own table and is it not therefore more than a memorial? And what justification is there for 'fencing it'? Are the two ordinances therefore not means of grace, perhaps 'special' means of grace, and therefore is not 'sacrament' a more appropriate word for baptism and the Lord's Supper than 'ordinance'.

Of course there are 'points of rest' and Welsh Baptists have held fast to Reformation doctrines, but like all other Christian institutions they are open to the promptings of the Spirit and to the pressures of changing historical situations. The Baptist craft may be soundly anchored, but it bobs about on the waves, sometimes carried by the currents of ebb and flow to the extreme length of the chain, at other times carried back to a position immediately above the anchorage. How widespread and how deep the changes are it is difficult to say, but no account of ourselves would be accurate or complete if it misses the signs of change. Welsh Baptists are not nearly as static as they appear to be both to themselves and others.

II. *Ourselves and Others*

With the rapid growth in the number of members and churches in the nineteenth century Baptists developed a lively denominational consciousness. This and their adherence to believer's baptism and a closed communion table left them open to the charge of exclusiveness. This is not surprising since there were and there are still those, fortunately in a minority, who tend to equate denial of the world with denial of fellowship with other Christians. There are others and they are in the majority, whose conviction that the historic catholic church is present in the local church compels them to give expression to this view of catholicity by reaching out in fellowship to other Christians.

Baptists have a long tradition of associating with one another. The autonomy of the local church has always co-existed with inter-dependence. At the earliest point in their story their church sought regular fellowship with one another for mutual encouragement and discipline. "The Association" is a significant component of Baptist structure, (there are fourteen such Associations in Wales at the present time) and when national Baptist Unions were formed in the nineteenth century they could be fairly described as the Associations associating with one another.

They have been happy to carry this 'principle of associating', if it may be so called, into their relationship with other communions. Thus they have always been active members of Free Church Councils at local, regional and national levels. They have been associated with the Council for Sunday Schools and Christian Education since its inception, they have been members of the Council of Churches for Wales and at University level they have shared with other communions in training for the ministry.

Indeed it would be difficult for the various communions to live in isolation of one another in a small country like Wales where there are few large towns and where villages and rural communities predominate. It seems as if providence has done all in his power to compel the churches in Wales to be aware of one another and to live together. Almost every community, however small, is served by two or more of the various church traditions, with their buildings standing cheek by jowl. It is not surprising therefore that there has been a long history of fellowship in worship and mutual help, of the sharing of buildings and pastoral concern and the emergence in recent years of community ministries.

Notwithstanding this growth in togetherness, the idea of organic incorporation in an united church or involvement in a federal structure finds little favour among Baptists. They are hesitant, fearing that incorporation would lead to relegation of believer's baptism to a secondary place with all that this implies for their understanding of church membership and the nature of the church. Moreover they are constrained by fear of a monolithic church order in which the individual could so easily and quickly degenerate into a position of perpetual spiritual adolescence. Nonetheless, for all their hesitations and fears,

Baptists would join with all God's people in affirming that the length and breadth, the height and depth of His love in Christ is to be comprehended only with all the saints.

III. *Ourselves and Our Mission*

Vows taken at believer's baptism carry with them the obligation of mission and therefore the task of evangelism is the privilege of all, not only of the specially gifted and full time 'professional'. The emphasis on the priesthood of all believers, so formly held by Baptists, requires a parallel emphasis on the apostolate of all believers. For Baptists evangelism means the proclamation of the good news of Christ with conversion as its aim, and it is in the light of this vocation to bring men to an acceptance of Christ as Saviour and King that they understand the very existence and purpose of the church.

The field is the world and Welsh Baptists have been happy to share with their English and Scottish counterparts in the work of the Baptist Missionary Society. The retreat of the people of Wales from the Faith has, however, made Wales as much of a Mission field as any overseas region, and Welsh Baptists are on record as stating that any evangelistic effort to meet this situation should in future be on an ecumenical basis.

Whilst they would give priority to the conversion of men and women, many Baptists would include the making of the social order more Christian in their vocation to evangelise. Their comprehensive conception of proclaiming the good news prompts them to identify themselves with movements for the relief of the disinherited and the oppressed, for the liberalising of human institutions, justice for prisoners of conscience, and with various peace and disarmament groups and fellowships.

Baptists in Wales, however, are acutely conscious how ill-equipped they are, morally and spiritually, for this huge task and how ineffective their efforts have been. They are sorrowfully and penitently aware that the conversion of men and women and human societies must begin with the renewal of themselves.

Church in Wales

Members: 136,000*   *Ministers: 725*   *Churches: 1,635*

* Easter Communicants

Response from the Church in Wales on its understanding of the nature and purpose of the Church

The Church in Wales came into being as an independent Province of the Anglican Communion on March 31st, 1920. This was as the result of an Act of Parliament which severed the four Welsh dioceses from the Church of England, thus taking away their status as part of the Established Church as well as all their ancient endowments. It became a self-governing church with a synodical pattern of government and with an Electoral College which elected its bishops. In the sixty-five years since Disestablishment the Church in Wales (C/W from here on) has been able to build up a strong sense of its identity and calling. It has become much more aware of its mission to the people of Wales than was possible when it was a group of dioceses of the Church of England occupying this particular part of the United Kingdom.

At this point let us briefly consider the setting in which the C/W ministers. When we refer to Wales we are not just referring to a geographical expression or a distinctive region of Britain but to a people with a sufficient sense of identity to qualify for the term 'nation', although being part of the unitary state of the United Kingdom. What once gave the people of Wales a unity was a separate shared language, but Welsh is now spoken by only 20% of the population, although it still has a vigorous cultural life with numerous publications and radio and T.V. programmes. There has been a great increase in the number of bilingual schools, and while there are many pressures on the language, its future, even if as a minority language, seems fairly assured. There is tension between the Welsh-speaking and non-Welsh-speaking communities, as the latter object to being classified as second class Welshpeople. Despite the absence of the language they have a strong sense of being Welsh. Yet political nationalism is not a strong force as evidenced by the Referendum of 1979 on the question of a Welsh Assembly which received comparatively little support. We seem to be going through a period of change. Politically, the Labour party, which has dominated in Wales for the last forty years, seems to be losing support amongst the people.

Industrially, the heavy industries of coal and steel which were paramount in industrial South Wales, have now greatly shrunk, and while more varied light industry has been introduced, unemployment is at a very high level. From being a country with a marked religious observance, with the main Non-conformist bodies being well supported, a recent survey claims that now only 13% of the population are regular worshippers. Through its adherence to the parochial system, the C/W seeks to minister to the whole people of Wales. It sees itself as having a special responsibility and vocation to serve the whole nation not just sections. It is itself committed to a bi-lingual policy (through its publications and in the deliberations of its Governing Body); most of the parishes in the Welsh speaking areas (which are mainly in the North and West) have Welsh services.

In discussing our understanding of our church, we take as a starting point a brief answer in the recently revised Catechism which is in our new Prayer Book. There the C/W is described as "the ancient Church of this land, catholic and reformed. It proclaims and holds fast to the doctrine and ministry of the One, Holy, Catholic and Apostolic Church". Clearly in this answer, the C/W sees itself as part of the universal Church, holding fast the doctrine and ministry of the undivided church. Anglicans claim to have no specific doctrines or confessional statements which are not found in the ancient church; typically, the summary of the Faith given in the Catechism is that provided by the Apostles and Nicene Creeds. The ministry referred to is the traditional three-fold ministry of bishops, priests and deacons, with an unbroken succession of bishops going back to the first founders of the sees. The same note of continuity is stressed when the C/W looks at its own history. It sees itself as 'the ancient church of this land', in continuity with the church of the Celtic saints and missionaries of the Dark Ages. This is given visible expression in that so many of our ancient churches are dedicated to the names of these saints, and often occupy the site of their cells and monastries. We are reminded of our continuity with the Middle Ages by the many medieval Parish and Abbey Churches which are still used for worship. The Catechism also reminds us that we are 'reformed'. At the Reformation medieval abuses and distortions were removed, and there was a return to the Scriptures as the main source of authority and to the Gospel as the source of salvation. There was also a return to worship in the vernacular. In Wales this meant a translation of prayer Book and Bible into Welsh, as well as into English.

If the whole section of the catechism is looked at, together with the teaching found elsewhere in the Prayer Book, the view of the church that emerges is that it consists of the whole company of God's people, called into being by God, founded on the life, death and resurrection of Our Lord, guided and quickened by the Holy Spirit. It is called to manifest the marks of oneness, catholicity, holiness and apostolicity. The doctrine of the Communion of Saints reminds us that the visible Church on earth is only part of the whole Church which spans death and includes both the living and the departed. The Church in Wales sees itself as part of this society.

It is a structured society. In commending this understanding to other denominations, the C/W in common with the rest of the Anglican Communion, sees as the only possible basis of unity the four elements which give the Church its structure and form, namely, the Bible as the rule and standard of faith, "containing all things necessary to salvation", the ancient Creeds as statements of the Faith, the two sacraments ordained by Christ himself – Baptism and the Eucharist, and the historic episcopate.

While the C/W holds no distinctive doctrine or practice apart from that belonging to the whole Anglican Communion, and to the whole Church, there is a distinctive ethos which distinguishes it from the other Anglican Provinces in Britain. We have already noted the different setting in which it ministers. It differs from the Church of England in being a small church, and in being completely free from State involvement in its appointments and governance. It differs from the Church of Ireland and the Episcopal Church of Scotland in that it is the largest Communion in Wales, not numerically dominated by large national churches as they are. Unlike the Church of England, it is, however, outnumbered by the Nonconformist denominations taken together. The six main denominational groupings in Wales can conveniently be divided into three which have a centralised denominational structure and three which are Unions of independent churches. Another possible division is provided by the language – three of the six are predominantly Welsh language churches. Owing to its smallness it lacks the diversity found in the Church of England, including, it might be said, pronounced party spirit or division. The smallness too has helped to promote a strong sense of fellowship and intimacy, although too it may occasion a certain insularity and even insecurity.

In considering the purpose of the Church in Wales, again the Catechism is helpful. "The mission of the church is to be the instrument of God in restoring all people to unity with God and each other in Christ ... it carries out its mission as it prays and worships, proclaims the Gospel and serves God's will in promoting justice, peace and love in all the world". This defines the purpose of the Church as continuing and extending the reconciling work of Christ, and accomplishing it through the traditional means of prayer and worship, proclamation and teaching, witness and service. The mission is entrusted to the whole people of God, and the laity must be encouraged and equipped to play a full part in this mission. The C/W sees its mission as primarily to the people of Wales, but it encourages its members, both clerical and lay, to offer themselves for work overseas, and so share in the Church's mission in other parts of the world. The C/W values highly its links with the Anglican Communion seeing the membership of this world wide family of churches as one of the ways in which a small province can acquire a vision and understanding of the world Church.

In turning to the relationship between the C/W and other Christian bodies in Wales, a historical perspective is important. Allusion has already been made to the fact that the C/W is outnumbered by the other denominations taken together. This discrepancy was far greater in the middle of the last century when Welsh Nonconformity was at its zenith. It resented the privileged status given to a minority church which it saw, with some justification, as lacking sympathy with Welsh needs and interests. It was this resentment which fuelled the campaign to disestablish the church which was strongly supported by the Liberal Party. As a result of this campaign, relations with the Nonconformists were strained and bitter in the early part of this century. It was not until after 1945 that the Ecumenical Movement began to have a real influence in Wales, and inter-church relations began to improve.

Apart from informal and personal contacts, the relation of the C/W with other Christian bodies on a national level can be thus classified:

(a) There is the relation with most other bodies within the Council of Churches for Wales. The Council itself has not been notably effective in influencing the life of the Churches, partly due to lack of resources (it has never had a full-time secretary since its inception in 1956), partly due to the diversity of views and churches it seeks to represent, and partly because the churches themselves have not delegated sufficiently to the Council; for instance, they have continued to produce reports on social issues within their own councils. The role of the Council in relation to the British Council of Churches also needs clarification. yet membership of the Council and its constituent Divisions and Committees have helped build up a network of relations and a growth in mutual trust and confidence which has helped change completely the ecumenical scene in Wales;

(b) The Council provided the base for the most serious and significant development in this scene, namely, the acceptance in 1975 of a Covenant to work and pray for the bringing in of one visible Church, by four of the denominations, the Presbyterian Church of Wales, the Methodist Church, the United Reformed Churches and the C/W. In 1977, ten churches in the Baptist Union of Great Britain entered into the Covenant. The Covenant consisted of seven articles, each of which was divided into two sections – the first referring to unity already recognised to exist and the second to the further agreement to be sought. Important things were said in the Covenant which had never been officially acknowledged before, e.g. "We recognise ... in one another the same faith in the gospel of Jesus Christ found in Holy Scripture ... the same awareness of God's calling to serve his gracious purpose for all mankind with particular responsibility for this land and people ... one another as within the one Church of Jesus Christ ... the ordained ministries of all our churches as true ministries of the word and sacraments." These terms mean that the C/W recognises that its Covenant partners share with it in the same mission to the people of Wales, that the schisms which exist are within the Church of God, and that consequently the grace of God through ministry and sacraments is truly at work within all the churches. At the same time the Covenant acknowledged that much had still to be done in reaching a common understanding and unity. The C/W differs perhaps in two main respects from its Covenant partners – in its emphasis on the centrality of the sacraments, especially the Eucharist, in the life of the Church, and on its doctrine of the ministry. These differences have helped to ensure that progress in implementing the Covenant and in enabling it to influence deeply the life and thinking of the churches has been slow. Nevertheless real progress has been acheived e.g. an agreed rite has been adopted for use at Joint Celebrations of the Eucharist, models of local church co-operation have been agreed, regular meetings of the bishops and the other leaders take place. The Commission of Covenanted Churches is now bringing to the churches a statement on the ministry and a method of reconciling the ministries which if accepted will lead to the unification of the churches in the forseeable future.

(c) There is the relation with the Roman Catholic Church in Wales. Again there has been some progress especially on the informal level. There have been a series of joint conferences and meetings, a joint Working Party has encouraged areas of co-operation and explored some of the points of difference. Since 1983 the bishops of the two churches meet regularly. The Roman Catholic Church has been considering the possibility of joining the Council of Churches for Wales. This event would be a great step forward in encouraging relations. Perhaps too some structure is needed to explore and stimulate fuller co-operation between the two churches.

This paper has attempted to describe briefly the Church in Wales' understanding of the nature and purpose of the Church. The last section has underlined the growing awareness that it cannot effectively present Christ to the people of Wales without co-operating with the other denominations. Its own commitment to unity and its visible manifestation is made clear in its acceptance of the Covenant. If some critics think that ecumenical progress in Wales has been negligible, they betray a lack of appreciation of the religious history of Wales. In the context of that history, progress in the last twenty years has been remarkable and offers considerable grounds for hope for the future.

D.H.J.
March 1986

Presbyterian Church of Wales (Calvanistic Methodist Church).

Members: 77,000   *Ministers: 200*   *Churches: 1,120*

1. A short declaration of Faith and Practice

With the whole Church in heaven and in earth we worship the one living and true God, Father, Son and Holy Spirit, perfect in love and holiness, in power and wisdom. Of Him, and through Him, and unto Him, are all things. To Him be the glory for ever.

It is the gracious will of God that all men should come to know Him, nor has He left Himself without witness in any age or nation. To the children of Israel He made known His Name, revealing Himself more and more as a just God and a Saviour. Unto us He speaks in His Son, giving us the light and the knowledge of His glory in the face of Jesus Christ. In Christ, we attain to the fulness of the knowledge of God and of His thoughts towards us. He that hath seen Him hath seen the Father.

In Jesus Christ God has accomplished the eternal purpose of His love by coming Himself to be the Saviour of men. Through Christ's perfect life in the flesh, His death for us on the Cross, His resurrection and His exaltation to the right hand of God, we have eternal redemption. Through faith in Him we are reconciled to God, delivered from sin, and made members of the family of God. In Him we are also reconciled one to another, and, constrained by His love, we learn to love and serve one another as the children of God. Thanks be to God for His unspeakable gift.

Through His Holy Spirit God fulfils the glorious purposes of His grace in Christ Jesus. Through the Spirit He dwells in them that believe, changing them into the likeness of Christ, and calling them to be His Holy Church, to glorify Christ in the world and to hasten the coming of His Kingdom. Through the Spirit, also, He leads believers into all truth, convinces the world and guides the ages, until the Kingdom come with power, when out Lord Jesus Christ shall be manifested in glory, and God shall be all in all.

Believing these things, we vow to be faithful to Christ: to seek daily to know the will of our Lord, and so to live that in all things we may be well pleasing in His sight; to confess Him before men; to proclaim His Gospel and further the ends of His Kingdom in all the world, until all men acknowledge Him as the one Saviour of the soul, the one Redeemer of society, the one King and Judge of all mankind.

We bless God for the Gospel of His Son and the manifold gifts of the Holy Spirit; for the Holy Scriptures and the Ministry of the Word; for the Sacraments and Ordinances of the Church; for the Fellowship of the Saints and the Communion with God; for the promise of a new heaven and a new earth wherein dwelleth Righteousness; and for the blessed hope of Life Eternal through Jesus Christ our Lord.

Now unto Him that is able to do exceeding abundantly above all that we ask or think, unto Him be the glory in the Church by Christ Jesus through all ages, world without end. Amen.

2. The Purpose of the Church

The purpose of the Church is to worship God and spread the Gospel of the Lord Jesus Christ as it is revealed in the Holy Scriptures and expounded in the doctrinal standards of the Church, through establishing and maintaining fellowships of people worshipping God and believing in the Lord Jesus Christ. The Church endeavours to attain this purpose by preaching the Gospel, administering the sacraments, pastoral oversight of the local churches, Christian fellowship and prayer, religious and scriptural instruction in the home, the Sunday school and similar organisations; by instructing communicants, preparation of literature, daily living, good works and service in the community and by setting apart certain persons for evangelising and working in special fields, together with any other means that the Church shall determine from time to time.

3. Relation to other Christian denominations

The Presbyterian Church of Wales has been in the forefront of ecumenical development in Wales. The Church has been a member of the Council of Churches for Wales from the very beginning and in 1974 convenanted with the Church of Wales, the Methodist Church, the United Reformed Church and churches belonging to the Baptist Union of Great Britain and Ireland to work and pray for unity. The Church also belongs to the Free Church Council for Wales, the National Free Church Federal Council (British), the British Council of Churches, the World Council of Churches and the World Alliance of Reformed Churches. Further, the Church is involved in an increasing number of local inter-Church and ecumenical projects involving the sharing of resources, buildings and ministers/clergymen. Church leaders in Wales meet regularly and from time to time take common action on social issues of mutual concern.

4. With other Churches in Wales the Presbyterian Church belongs to the 'Wales for Christ' Committee, the purpose of which is to initiate and develop united action to further mission within Wales. The Church is also a member of the Council for World Mission to which belong 32 Churches of the Reformed tradition in Africa, the Caribbean regions, East and South Asia, the Pacific as well as the United Kingdom and the Netherlands.

Union of Welsh Independants

Members: 62,500   *Ministers: 195*   *Churches: 700*

The Testimony of the Union of Welsh Independents

In seeking to convey our understanding of the nature and purpose of our churches we, who belong to the Union of Welsh Independents, have to begin with Him whose we truly are, the Lord Jesus Christ, and with His crowned rights. The Church is His work and He is her only Foundation and Head. It is He who is to govern her life, and this He does through the light of the Word and the leading of His Spirit. The chief purpose of the Church is to extol her Lord, to express His Life and to witness to His Kingdom.

We are led to believe that certain basic principles are implied in this.

1. A church becomes visible whenever and wherever persons come together to enthrone Christ as Lord and to wait upon Him. Gathering together to worship and to seek the mind of God in Christ is the essential activity of a church.

2. This gathering together is an entirely voluntary act. In our view it is entirely erroneous to identify a church with the inhabitants of a parish or the subjects of a state. We wholeheartedly adhere to our fathers' description of a church in terms of covenant. We are people who have covenanted together in the presence of the Lord to walk together in accordance with His Word, as the Holy Spirit gives us light.

We believe that the church, the covenanted congregation, has a form and an order which differentiate it from other institutions. We should like to think that the system adopted by us in accordance with the Gospel, as in its emphasis on a definite ministry of ministers and deacons, in the freedom of every member to contribute, as the Holy Spirit urges him, to the ordering of the church by means of the Church Meeting, and in church membership founded on personal confession.

3. Since Christ Himself promises His presence to those who meet in His name, the life of a church is complete in Him. There is nothing of essential importance that a local church can receive apart from Him who bestows upon it grace after grace. It cannot reach a higher degree of completeness by any secular or religious plan or organisation.

4. We believe that the ministry of Christ in His Church is such that the whole congregation with its variety of gifts can participate in it on equal terms. It is thus that we understand the priesthood of all believers and so we cannot see that there is room for an order of priests or clergy in the Church of Christ. We are all servants of Christ the Servant and it is our privilege to serve one another for His sake. 'One who serves' is a minister or a deacon, as suggested by the orginal meaning of these words.

We give due dignity to the ministry of the Word and the Sacraments, ensuring that the divine call to this work is confirmed by more than one church and that a person who is to be recognised for this responsibility receives a full theological education. In our view there is no male or female in this special ministry. We do not restrict the ministry of the Sacraments to those who have been ordained but we regard it as entirely acceptable that where no ordained minister is available the church may invite one of its own number to baptize or preside at the communion table.

5. Acknowledging the lordship of Christ in His Church we cannot yield the authority to any other, be it institution or person. We consider that the truest way to acknowledge His authority is for the prayerful congregation to depend not on the judgement or whim of a majority of its members but on the mind of Christ as revealed by the Word and the Spirit. This for us is the significance and importance of a Church Meeting. It is our deep conviction that a Church Meeting is of necessity entirely independent of all state institutions and ecclesiastical organisations.

This 'Independency' is not of the flesh but is a lofty spiritual principle. It does not mean a selfish isolationism. Since Christ manifests Himself in the life of His people everywhere, every church must be conscious of this 'life' as it finds expression in other churches. In the liberty of Christ and under the impulse of His love every company of His people is led to co-operate eagerly with other companies, and this on a local, national and international scale.

Independents have been led not only to co-operate with each other in Association and Union and a World Fellowship but also to join with other denominations in activities like those of the World Council of Churches and the British Council of Churches.

6. We believe that the lordship of Christ is to be acknowledged not only in worship but also in life and that the Church as it spreads in the world is called to be salt and light. It is its privilege to speak of Him and to act in His name. This means a refusal to conform to the world, and, if necessary, in seeking to promote the revolution of the Kingdom. conflict with the principalities and powers. We feel a special responsibility in all this to contribute to the social witness of the Gospel within Wales and to emphasise, in the age of the arms race, the superiority of the way of reconciliation.

As we present our understanding of the nature and purpose of a church, we are very conscious of our failure to be faithful to the truth as we see it. We fully understand that this truly lofty conception of the nature of a church is one unquestionably difficult to realise. Without continual submision and obedience to Christ and without the light of His Spirit our 'independency' can become a selfish religion and we may set store by human rather than seeking prayerfully for the mind of Christ.

All our experiences in putting into practice the Independent and Congregational way serve to underline our dependence upon the grace of God and bid us bear in mind the great Protestant principle that the Church must always be open to be reformed anew.

In our relationship with other denominations we rejoice to see significant indications that the congregational element within them is being strengthened. We realise at the same time that the bonds connecting our churches with each other are becoming much stronger. There is inevitable tension between the need to safeguard the identity of the local church and the urge to promote the co-operation of all the churches; but we recognise that this is a creative tension and can be a growth-point in our history.

In respect of mission at home and abroad we appreciate the growing opportunities that come to us to bear common witness with other denominations and we rejoice in all progress in inter-denominational endeavours. In respect of mission on a world scale we can participate with the Presbyterian Church of Wales in the work of the Council for World Mission. Our membership of the World Council of Churches, the British Council of Churches and the Free Church Federal Council gives us a wide ecumenical dimension. Nearer home we have played our part in the Council of Evangelical Churches in Wales, the Welsh Sunday Schools Council and the United Missionary Council for Wales. We have been a member of the Welsh Council of Churches from the start and we take pride in the prominent contribution of several of our members to its work. It was the vision of one of our ministers that led to the 'Wales for Christ' campaign and this mission work remains to remind us that the winning of Wales – and indeed of the world – to the kingdom of Jesus is work for all of us and work for us to do together.

Although the Union of Welsh Independents did not see their way clear to unite in 'A Covenant towards Union', we too have our concern for the keeping of the unity which is given by the Spirit. We humbly believe that the conception of the nature of a church cherished by us is one which all the denominations could appropriately consider in all seriousness in their quest for unity. We should like to think that our loyalty to this conception could be no small contribution to the present ecumenical dialogue.

We know of course that making our contribution is not our

only privilege. It will be our privilege also to receive what our fellow Christians of all traditions have to give and to be enriched by their experiences.

We pray that the Spirit of Truth will cause more light to break forth from His Word to lead us all into the years that are ahead.

List of Churches Participating in the Inter-Church Process 'Not Strangers But Pilgrims!'

ENGLAND
African Methodist Episcopal Church
Baptist Union of Great Britain and Ireland
Calvary Church of God in Christ
Christian Brethren
Church of England
Congregational Federation
Council of African and Allied Churches
Greek Orthodox Church
Independent Methodist Churches
Lutheran Council of Great Britain
Methodist Church in Great Britain
    (including the Synods of Scotland and Shetlands)
Moravian Church in Great Britain and Ireland
New Testament Assembly
Old Baptist Union
Religious Society of Friends (Quakers)
Roman Catholic Church in England and Wales
Russian Orthodox Church
Salvation Army
Seventh Day Adventists
Shiloh United Church of Christ
Unitarian and Free Christian Churches
United Reformed Church
Wesleyan Holiness Church

SCOTLAND
Church of Scotland
Congregational Union of Scotland
Scottish Episcopal Church
Roman Catholic Church in Scotland
United Free Church of Scotland

WALES
Baptist Union of Wales
Church in Wales
Prebyterian Church in Wales
Union of Welsh Independants